Israel in Bible Prophecy
The New Testament Fulfillment of the Promise to Abraham

By Brian Godawa

Israel in Bible Prophecy: The New Testament Fulfillment of the Promise to Abraham
2nd Edition c

Copyright © 2017, 2021 Brian Godawa
All rights reserved. No part of this book may be reproduced in any form or by any electronic or mechanical means, including information storage and retrieval systems, without prior written permission, except in the case of brief quotations in critical articles and reviews.

Warrior Poet Publishing
www.warriorpoetpublishing.com

ISBN: 978-1-942858-37-9 (paperback)

Scripture quotations taken from *The Holy Bible: English Standard Version.* Wheaton: Standard Bible Society, 2001, except where noted as the NASB: *New American Standard Bible: 1995 Update.* (LaHabra, CA: The Lockman Foundation, 1995).

Dedicated to
The fans of *Chronicles of the Apocalypse*

Table of Contents

1 Who Are the Children of Abraham? 5
2 Father of Many Nations 10
3 Children of Abraham 14
4 Everlasting Covenant 20
5 Land Promise 22
6 Conditional Covenant 33
7 Circumcision 42
8 The Temple 47
9 Blessing and Cursing 54
10 The Regathering of Israel 56
11 Old Testament Shadow, New Testament Reality 87
Get the Theology behind Chronicles of the Apocalypse . 966
Get More Biblical Imagination 98
Chronicles of the Nephilim 99
Chronicles of the Apocalypse 100
Chronicles of the Watchers 101
About The Author 102

1
Who Are the Children of Abraham?

Many Christians believe that the Jews of today are still God's "chosen people." Yet most of these same Christians maintain that personal salvation can only be received through faith in Jesus Christ. They hold to the belief that God still has a special plan for the geographical entity of Israel and those they believe are the physical descendants of Abraham.

Every day, prophecy pundits in the media exegete newspapers tirelessly proclaiming that current world events "are all prophesied right in the Bible" and now being fulfilled "right before our eyes." They've been doing this for over 170 years, changing their interpretations as their predictions failed to occur. Prophetic speculation is upgraded and updated for the next go-round. The merchandisers of prophecy know that sizeable financial rewards can come from the right kind of alarming message in what has become a business I call the Bible Prophecy Industrial Complex. Millions of dollars flows into the coffers of prophecy ministries every year through conferences, books, dvds, and other media, teaching their peculiar viewpoints in relation to newspaper headlines. This kind of big business Bible preaching can be corrupting, through blurring motives and creating a need for constant sensationalism, that often vulgarizes the real intent of prophetic passages, completely out of their original contexts.

The dominant prophetic scheme, usually called Dispensationalism (and it's grandfather, Premillennialism), teaches that the modern ethnic or genetic people called Jews and their modern geopolitical land called Israel are still the center of God's redemptive plan because, after all, God made a promise to Abraham about multiplying his descendants and giving them the Promised Land, and God isn't about to change his mind. Dispensationalists cite Exodus 32:13 where God says to Moses:

> Exodus 32:13
> "Remember Abraham, Isaac, and Israel, your servants, to whom you swore by your own self, and said to them, 'I will multiply your offspring as the stars of heaven, and all this land that I have promised I will give to your offspring, and they shall inherit it forever.' "

This verse says that God's promise of inheritance to Abraham's offspring is "forever," so it logically follows that it is still in effect, right? After all, God doesn't fall back on his promises. So, He must still be intent upon giving a physical Israel that physical land He promised so long ago, or else God is a liar, right?

Wrong. This Dispensational viewpoint is not merely unbiblical, it is a serious negation of the glorious New Covenant that God established with the coming of Messiah/Christ. Dispensationalists advanced their novel belief, after 1800 years of church history, that God has two separate plans, one for Israel after the flesh and one for the New Testament Church after the spirit. So they attempt to maintain special status for Israel while also affirming the New Covenant. It's as if God has two covenants, one with the Jews and one with the Church. But this attempt at simultaneous plans for different "people of God" is ultimately a repudiation of the very concept of the New Covenant in Christ that has abolished all distinction between Jew and Gentile. To say that the physical descendants of Abraham are God's chosen people *after* Messiah has come and *fulfilled* the Old Covenant types and shadows is to negate the New Covenant itself and replace it with a return to the types and shadows that it has replaced.

At about this point, a common knee jerk reaction assumes that such a viewpoint is "anti-Semitic" bringing on some future persecution of the Jews, a "road to holocaust" as one merchandiser of prophecy proclaimed. Well nothing could be further from the truth. Let me state at the outset that I support the modern state of Israel's right to exist and right to kill terrorist peoples and nations whose sole intent is to "drive the Jews into the sea," (obliterating them as a people and a nation). I believe modern Israel is a legitimate sovereign nation and has every moral and legal right to self-defense against the tyranny of Muslim oppression that surrounds Israel and seeks to destroy her. I support the modern state of Israel because she is the sole representative democratic ally of the United States in the Middle East surrounded by monstrous tyranny. And I consider the anti-Semitism of Left Wing politics that demonizes Israel to be itself a revival of demonic Nazi thought patterns.

But a moral right to the land is not the same thing as a "divine right" to the land. And to understand that difference, we must see what God himself says about the promise to Abraham.

The Promise

Exodus 32:13 is really a reference to the original promise God made to Abraham in Genesis. Let's take a look at it and see what we can learn:

> Genesis 17:4–10
> "Behold, my covenant is with you, and you shall be the father of a multitude of nations. [5] No longer shall your name be called Abram, but your name shall be Abraham, for I have made you the father of a multitude of nations. [6] I will make you exceedingly fruitful, and I will make you into nations, and kings shall come from you. [7] And I will establish my covenant between me and you and your offspring after you throughout their generations for an everlasting covenant, to be God to you and to your offspring after you. [8] And I will give to you and to your offspring after you the land of your sojournings, all the land of Canaan, for an everlasting possession, and I will be their God." [9] And God said to Abraham, "As for you, you shall keep my covenant, you and your offspring after you throughout their generations. [10] This is my covenant, which you shall keep,

between me and you and your offspring after you: Every male among you shall be circumcised.

Now, what we see here are several elements to the one Promise made to Abraham by God. One, He will be a father of many nations (v 5). Two, the Promise is to Abraham and his offspring (literally: *seed*), which is stressed over and over throughout the passage (v 7). Three, it is an everlasting covenant, one that does not change (v 7). Four, Abraham's descendants shall inherit the land of Canaan, the land of Promise (v 8). Five, the covenant is conditioned upon their obedience (v 9). Six, the covenant is sealed by circumcision (v 10).

1) Father of many nations
2) Children of Abraham
3) Everlasting Covenant
4) Land Promise
5) Conditional Covenant
6) Circumcision

What I want to show is that each and every one of these elements of the Promise made to Abraham, is shown in the Scriptures to be fulfilled completely in Christ and his spiritual international body on earth, *not in a physical or geographical nation of Israel.*

Some have called this by the pejorative title, "Replacement Theology," as if God replaces Israel with the Church. But while this vulgar oversimplification may be helpful in targeting a Straw Man easy to take down, it does not reflect what the Bible is actually saying nor what I am saying. It is not a replacement that occurs, but rather a fulfillment and transformation in Christ that results in an exclusion of those who mistakenly consider themselves part of the Promise.

In short, from the beginning, God always intended that those who are of faith are his true Chosen People, not those who are of physical descent from Abraham. God's Promise to Abraham is fulfilled and applied to those who are *in Christ*, and the seal of that covenant is circumcision of the Spirit, not of the flesh.

> 2 Corinthians 1:20–22
>
> For all the promises of God find their Yes in him…And it is God who establishes us with you in Christ, and has anointed us, and who has also put his seal on us and given us his Spirit in our hearts as a guarantee.

But I'm getting ahead of myself. Let's start from the beginning.

2
Father of Many Nations

> Genesis 17:4–5 (NKJV)
>
> "As for Me, behold, My covenant is with you, and you shall be a father of many nations. [5] No longer shall your name be called Abram, but your name shall be Abraham; for I have made you a father of many nations."

> Genesis 26:4
>
> [4] I will multiply your offspring as the stars of heaven and will give to your offspring all these lands. And in your offspring all the nations of the earth shall be blessed."

It is common to misunderstand this promise of blessing to the nations as meaning that Israel will become an exalted geopolitical entity sometime in our future, and therefore a shining example to the Gentiles to join or emulate. As if they will remain a separated people from the other nations. But this view is mistaken, because God was not referring to the physical generation of peoples from Abraham's loins, but to the spiritual regeneration of peoples through faith. Look at how the New Testament declares how this promise was actually fulfilled:

> Romans 4:13–18
>
> [13] For the promise to Abraham and his offspring that he would be heir of the world did not come through the law but through the righteousness of faith. [14] For if it is the adherents of the law who are to be the heirs, faith is null and the promise is void. [15] For the law brings wrath, but where there is no law there is no transgression. [16] That is why it depends on faith, in order that the promise may rest on grace and be guaranteed to all his offspring—not only to the adherent of the law but also to the one who shares the faith of Abraham, who is the father of us all, [17] <u>as it is written, "I have made you the father of many nations"</u>... [18] In hope he believed against hope, that he should

become the father of many nations, as he had been told, "So shall your offspring be."

Notice that Paul is saying that the promise to Abraham's descendants is fulfilled "through the righteousness of faith," *not* through the Law (or Torah, which was the distinguishing mark of being Israel). In Romans 3 and 4, he makes the case that the physical Jew who received the Law of God and circumcision is not at an advantage over the Gentile because *all* are under sin. The Law cannot make the Jew righteous, but can only reveal sin and drive one to faith in Christ. By the time Paul gets to Abraham in chapter 4, he shows that even Abraham himself was not made righteous through the act of circumcision, but through his faith which he had *while being an uncircumcised Gentile.*

Therefore, God's promise of **multiplying descendants and being a father of many nations** is explicitly declared by Paul to be fulfilled through the righteousness of faith (the New Covenant), not through physical generation. He goes so far as to say in verse 14 that if the inheritance was through the Law made to the physical Jews, then the promise would actually be nullified! "Those who are of the faith of Abraham" (v. 16) are the inheritors, not mere physical descendants. Abraham's descendants are believing Christians, both Jew and Gentile, not unbelieving Jews.

The complaint may arise that verse 16 indicates God maintains separate relations or two different covenants with the physical Jews and Gentile believers. Doesn't the verse say, "in order that the promise may be certain to all the descendants, **not only** those who are of the Law, **but also** to those who are of the faith of Abraham, who is the father of us all"? So are there not two lines of descendants, physical and spiritual?

Not in context. Don't forget Paul's main point that just because the physical Jews received the Law and were circumcised, does not make them righteous or even Abraham's children. He is trying to show that *faith* is the common denominator between the Jewish believer and the Gentile believer.

> Romans 3:29–30
> Or is God the God of Jews only? Is he not the God of Gentiles also? Yes, of Gentiles also, ³⁰ since God is one—<u>who will justify the circumcised by faith and the uncircumcised through faith</u>.

So Paul is trying to explain that just because one is a physical Jew and has been circumcised, does not mean he is righteous or saved. The circumcised ***must also have faith***. So in the verse just before the controversial one we are discussing, he explains what he means by saying,

> Romans 4:12
> and to make him the father of the circumcised who are not merely circumcised but who also walk in the footsteps of the faith that our father Abraham had before he was circumcised.

So he is not talking about two plans in verse 16, one for Jews and one for Gentiles, he is not saying that there are two peoples of God through two different physical identities, but rather that the two physical identities are irrelevant, and they are one entity through faith in Christ. The circumcised Jew must not only have the Law (circumcision) but ***must also have faith*** or Abraham is not his father.

In the book of Galatians, Paul writes to Christians who have been hoodwinked into thinking that they must add to their faith an obedience to the distinctive laws of Jewish identity, or they are not saved. He addresses the very same Genesis Promise to Abraham and blessing of the nations by explaining that the blessing of the nations was not in Jewish identity but in faith. All the nations are blessed through justification by faith in Jesus Christ, not by a physical Israel with worldly power and glory.

> Galatians 3:8–9
> And the Scripture, foreseeing that God would justify the Gentiles by faith, preached the gospel beforehand to Abraham,

saying, "<u>In you shall all the nations be blessed</u>." [9] So then, those who are of faith are blessed along with Abraham, the man of faith.

Paul is very clear that "In you shall all the nations be blessed," means Gentiles will be justified through the faith of Abraham, not through his loins or through a national Israel separate from the Gentiles. Abraham is the father of Gentiles who come from all the nations and believe in Jesus Christ.

This is not to say that Gentiles alone are who God is saving or justifying, but rather *both* Jew *and* Gentile who believe. There is no favor of one over the other, there is only favor of those who believe. And those who believe are from "every nation, from all tribes and peoples and languages" (Rev 7:9). That is how Abraham is a father of many nations. He is the father of those who have faith from all the nations.

Which leads us to the second element of the Promise fulfilled.

3
Children of Abraham

> Genesis 17:7
> And I will establish my covenant between me and you and your offspring after you throughout their generations for an everlasting covenant, to be God to you and to your offspring after you.

The second part of God's promise to Abraham "and your offspring after you throughout their generations..." is really another aspect of the first element of Abraham being the father of many nations. But I have separated it out because it is the basis of the concept "seed of Abraham" or "children of Abraham" that is frequently referred to in the Older and Newer Covenants. What I want to prove here is that the Abrahamic "offspring" God is referring to was never the mere physical offspring of flesh, but has always been the spiritual offspring of faith.

In Galatians, Paul writes about the Judaizers, or the "party of the circumcision" (Gal 2:12). These men were saying to Gentile believers that they must become Jews in addition to their faith by bearing the physical marker of circumcision or they would not be considered the true sons of Abraham (Gal 2:4; 5:1-6). The Judaizers were affirming the special status of the physically circumcised Jews as sons of Abraham, sons of the Promise, the receivers of "the blessing." But Paul violently disagreed by explaining that *it is faith that makes one a son of Abraham to receive the promised blessing, not genetic or Jewishness according to the flesh.*

Galatians 3:6–9

⁶ just as Abraham "believed God, and it was counted to him as righteousness"? ⁷ Know then that it is those of faith who are the sons of Abraham. ⁸ And the Scripture, foreseeing that God would justify the Gentiles by faith, preached the gospel beforehand to Abraham, saying, "In you shall all the nations be blessed." ⁹ So then, those who are of faith are blessed along with Abraham, the man of faith.

So here again, that same Abrahamic promise from Genesis is quoted as being made to those of faith, ***not flesh***. He explicitly says that "those who are of faith are sons of Abraham," "those who are of faith are blessed with Abraham." He says that it was the promise *of faith* that was preached to Abraham when he made the Promise of all nations and descendants. There could be no clearer proof that God has always meant faith as the means of sonship, not flesh or physical descent or Jewish identity markers.

But just in case, the Dispensationalist can't see the obvious, Paul goes further to explain that the promise made to the offspring ("seed") of Abraham was to the singular person of Christ, not the plural people of the land.

Galatians 3:16

Now the promises were made to Abraham and to his offspring. It does not say, "And to offsprings," referring to many, but referring to one, "And to your offspring," who is Christ.

The word that we have translated as "offspring" is also translated as "seed," but the point remains the same. So Paul writes that all those promises—all six points of the covenant—that were made to Abraham, were really made to Christ (singular), NOT the physical descendants (plural). According to God's Word, Jesus Christ is *the* Seed of Abraham to whom the Promise was made. It could not be clearer.

He then equates "sons of Abraham" with "sons of God." We partake of that Abrahamic Promise by being "in Christ" through our faith.

Galatians 3:26–29

> [26] for in Christ Jesus you are all sons of God, through faith. [27] ...for you are all one in Christ Jesus. [29] And if you are Christ's, then you are Abraham's offspring, heirs according to promise.

Notice the last line. Abraham's offspring, those who are heirs of the promise to Abraham, are not the physical descendants of flesh, but the faithful in Christ. We believers inherit the Promise made to Abraham! The Promise of inheritance was never intended by God to refer to a genetic or nation state of Israel, but to the faithful in Christ. Now, of course, the faithful Jewish believers in the Old and New Testaments are included in that Promise (The OT believer looked forward to Messiah, the NT believer looks backward to Messiah), but both Jew and Gentile are included in the Promise through faith! The point is that there is no special status for a physical Israel of flesh in God's plan. Never was. It was always the faithful to whom God was making the Promise.

Later in the same book of Galatians, Paul takes this dichotomy of faithful versus physical farther and makes the separation even more stark. This passage is particularly indicting against the Dispensationalist because Paul talks specifically about the difference between fleshly Israel and faithful Israel, and stresses that fleshly Israel is never what God's promise was all about. Paul allegorically likens physical Israel ("according to the flesh") with the physical Jerusalem that was in slavery in the first century and the physical descendants of Hagar as the symbol of those fleshly offspring. Then he likens the faithful believers to the heavenly Jerusalem that he calls free, and it is these free faithful that are the inheritors of the promise, *not* the physical nation.

Galatians 4:22–26

> [22] For it is written that Abraham had two sons, one by a slave woman and one by a free woman. [23] But the son of the slave was born according to the flesh, while the son of the free woman was born through promise. [24] Now this may be interpreted allegorically: these women are two covenants. One

is from Mount Sinai, bearing children for slavery; she is Hagar. [25] Now Hagar is Mount Sinai in Arabia; she corresponds to the present Jerusalem, for she is in slavery with her children. [26] But the Jerusalem above is free, and she is our mother.

The "children of promise" are here spoken of as definitively being those who are of faith, *not* those who are physical Jews "according to the flesh." In fact, Paul writes that the physical Jews who were persecuting the Christians during his lifetime were those "fleshly" slaves of Hagar:

> Galatians 4:29
> [29] But just as at that time he who was born according to the flesh persecuted him who was born according to the Spirit, so also it is now.

And then he concludes by saying that the physical Jews who do not have faith in Christ will not inherit the Promise along with the faithful:

> Galatians 4:30–31
> [30] But what does the Scripture say? "Cast out the slave woman and her son, for the son of the slave woman shall not inherit with the son of the free woman." [31] So, brothers, we are not children of the slave but of the free woman.

There could be no stronger denial that the physical Jewish descendants will inherit the Promise of Abraham. According to Scripture, it isn't going to happen. The physical descendants "shall not be an heir" with the faithful sons of Abraham. Not in Paul's time, not in the future. There are not two plans, one for believing Gentiles and one for physical Jews. Only Jews who believe in Messiah will inherit the Promise *along with* the believing Gentiles. **Believers alone** are the "children of promise." God's promise to Abraham is not to Israel of the flesh, but to Israel of faith (that includes both Jew and Gentile).

> Galatians 4:23
> [23] But the son of the slave was born according to the flesh, while the son of the free woman was born through promise… [28] Now you, brothers, like Isaac, are children of promise.

And this brings us to another passage, Romans 9, which also speaks of Isaac and the continuation of the Promise to Abraham's offspring. Yet, here again, the distinction is made that God's Promise to Abraham was *not* to fleshly descendants of Abraham, but to faithful believers *like* Abraham:

> Romans 9:3–8
>
> [3] For I could wish that I myself were accursed and cut off from Christ for the sake of my brothers, my kinsmen according to the flesh. [4] They are Israelites, and to them belong the adoption, the glory, the covenants, the giving of the law, the worship, and the promises. [5] To them belong the patriarchs, and from their race, according to the flesh, is the Christ, who is God over all, blessed forever. Amen. [6] But it is not as though the word of God has failed. For not all who are descended from Israel belong to Israel, [7] and not all are children of Abraham because they are his offspring, but "Through Isaac shall your offspring be named." [8] This means that it is not the children of the flesh who are the children of God, but the children of the promise are counted as offspring.

Paul notes that physical Israel ("according to the flesh") were given the adoption, the glory, the covenants, Law, temple *and promises*. But then he states that nevertheless, not all fleshly descendants of Israel are actually Israel. Just because people were born in the physical line of Abraham does not make them Israel. Why? Because "children of the flesh are not the children of God, but the children of the promise are regarded as offspring!" And who has Paul established are "children of the promise" in Galatians and elsewhere? Believers!! Believers are the descendants of Abraham and Isaac, and children of the promise, NOT physical Jews "according to the flesh."

It seems to be a theme of Paul to hammer home this idea that God's promises were never made to physical descendants of Abraham, but rather to a spiritual remnant of true believers **within** the community of physical descendants. With the inauguration of the New Covenant, the "other sheep not of this fold" (Gentiles who also believe) are *now included* in on that Promise. The righteous has always lived by faith. God's promise was never made to physical Israel, but to "spiritual" Israel, or those with faith. This is why the Gentile believer is a true Jew, and a circumcised *unbelieving* fleshly Jew is not:

> Romans 2:28–29
> [28] For no one is a Jew who is merely one outwardly, nor is circumcision outward and physical. [29] But a Jew is one inwardly, and circumcision is a matter of the heart, by the Spirit, not by the letter. His praise is not from man but from God.

To conclude then, we see the New Testament go out of its way to stress that the offspring of Abraham, the "children of Abraham" to whom God made his promises, **are not** the physical Jews in the geographical land now called Israel, but are in fact all believers, both Jew and Gentile, not bound by any land. This is what Paul means when he says in Ephesians 2:14 that Christ "made both groups into one, and broke down the barrier of the dividing wall, by abolishing in His flesh the enmity, which is the Law of commandments contained in ordinances, that in Himself He might make the two into one new man."

We simply cannot divide Jew from Gentile in God's promise or plan as the Dispensationalist would want. Jew and Gentile *believers* are one in Christ and cannot be separated because that which separated them (The Laws of separation in the OT) has been abolished. To say that God has a separate plan for unbelieving physical Jews who reject Jesus as Messiah is to deny the very fulfillment of God's promise to true Israel, the spiritual unity of Jew and Gentile who believe in Jesus.

4
Everlasting Covenant

> Genesis 17:7
> And I will establish my covenant between me and you and your offspring after you throughout their generations for an everlasting covenant, to be God to you and to your offspring after you.

This third element of the Abrahamic Promise made by God is often a lynch pin for Dispensationalists because it appears to them that this substantiates the fact that even though the New Testament has arrived, it does not change a promise that is made "everlasting" to Abraham's offspring. This is why the Dispensationalist believes that there are two plans, one for the New Covenant and one for the "eternal promise" of the Old Covenant. Well, by now it is clear that this writer is fully in support of the eternality of God's promise. Yes, God keeps his promises, and if he says it is an everlasting covenant, it is.

But *how* he keeps his promises is sadly too often misunderstood, and to whom that everlasting covenant is made is misattributed by Dispensationalists. As I already argued above, the Children of Abraham, Abraham's offspring, are not physical descendants from his loins, but rather those who have faith in Jesus Christ. So New Covenant believers in Jesus are precisely those children of Abraham to whom God is still eternally fulfilling those promises. The New Covenant *is* the continuation of God's eternal promise of inheritance to Abraham's Seed:

> Hebrews 9:15
> Therefore [Jesus] is the mediator of a new covenant, so that those who are called may receive the promised eternal inheritance.

Yes, the promise is eternal, it's just not inherited by physically circumcised Jews, but by believers in Christ. According to the Scriptures, New Testament believers are the ones receiving God's everlasting covenant made to Abraham of an everlasting inheritance.

And what is that inheritance, but the land of Promise, the land of Canaan? Again, this inheritance is misunderstood by many. So let's conquer that promised land next.

5
Land Promise

Genesis 17:8

[8] "And I will give to you [Abraham] and to your offspring after you the land of your sojournings, all the land of Canaan, for an everlasting possession, and I will be their God."

So why did God promise Abraham the land of Canaan? Was it just a kind of territory grab? In order to understand what this "inheritance" thing is all about, we must go way back to the tower of Babel. Here is what Moses wrote about that incident:

Deuteronomy 32:8–9

[8] When the Most High gave to the nations their inheritance, when he divided mankind, he fixed the borders of the peoples according to the number of the sons of God. [9] But the LORD's portion is his people, Jacob his allotted heritage.

This passage shows the origin of the inheritance of land ("heritage") being at the Tower of Babel. Mankind had been united in evil with their pursuit of idolatry and self-deification ("let us make a name for ourselves"). Genesis 10 gives us the seventy nations that came out of that Babel incident. And Moses writes that the borders of those nations were established, and rebellious humanity was given over to the authority of the sons of God.

Who are these sons of God? While there is disagreement over this question, I have argued in my book *When Giants Were Upon the Earth,* that they were in fact, the rebel divine beings who fell to earth during the days of Noah.

So why would God allot Gentile nations to those fallen angelic beings? Because they refused to worship Yahweh, and continued to worship other gods. Another Deuteronomy passage clarifies this allotment of the Gentiles to false gods.

> Deuteronomy 4:19–20
>
> [19] And beware lest you raise your eyes to heaven, and when you see the sun and the moon and the stars, all the host of heaven, you be drawn away and bow down to them and serve them, <u>things that the LORD your God has allotted to all the peoples under the whole heaven</u>. [20] But the LORD has taken you and brought you out of the iron furnace, out of Egypt, to be a people <u>of his own inheritance</u>, as you are this day.

In the ancient world, people considered the stars to be both signs in the heavens as well as gods. They called them "host of heaven" because they believed them to be divine beings who resided in the heavens. So God is saying that he "allotted" those Gentile nations to their false gods as their inheritance. The false gods were spiritual authorities over fallen mankind and their geographical territories.

At the same time, and in the same way, God allotted the offspring of Abraham to be his inheritance, and their territory would be the land of Canaan. So the concept of inheritance was tightly wound into the notion of land and the spiritual territorial authority over that land. The book of Daniel calls these territorial spiritual powers, "Watchers," and "Princes" over nations (Dan 4:13, 21; 10:13, 20-21).

So when God promised Abraham the land of Canaan as his inherited possession, he was merely updating his original land allotment made at Babel. The title deeds to the rest of the earth were in the hands of the Watchers, the fallen sons of God. But God held the title deed to Canaan for Israel's inheritance. This was why inheriting land and keeping it within the tribes of Israel was so important in God's Law. It was all about maintaining that allotment, that promised inheritance.

But something else also happened on the way to the New Covenant. The notion of Israel's inheritance was transformed from a local land of Canaan into all the earth because of Messiah.

Psalm 2:7–8

⁷ I will tell of the decree: The LORD said to me, "You are my Son; today I have begotten you. ⁸ Ask of me, and I will make the nations your heritage, and <u>the ends of the earth your possession</u>.

Messiah would take the title deed of land away from the false gods of the nations and would end up inheriting, not merely Canaan, but all the earth. This is in fact what Jesus did in his death, resurrection and ascension: he defeated the evil principalities and powers over the nations, took back their title deeds, and led them in a triumphal march of victory over them (Col 2:15; Eph 4:8). Now people of every tribe and nation would be God's inheritance, and he would be theirs. Jesus destroyed the separation between Jew and Gentile nations (Eph 2:11-22). The inheritance of God's people is no longer a single plot of land in the Middle East called Israel, it is all the earth because God's people are from all the earth, all the nations.

Have you ever wondered why there is no more literal or direct references to the land inheritance in the New Testament? Because of the New Covenant, the localized nationalistic land inheritance has necessarily been redirected by God into spiritual fulfillment in Christ. The kingdom of God is the Land of Promise in Christ. Our inheritance as the people of God is not a physical piece of land, but a heavenly land, not an earthly kingdom, but a spiritual kingdom, the kingdom of God (1Cor 15:50).

1 Peter 1:3–4

³ He has caused us to be born again to a living hope through the resurrection of Jesus Christ from the dead, ⁴ <u>to an inheritance that is imperishable, undefiled, and unfading, kept in heaven for you.</u>

Hebrews 9:15

¹⁵ Therefore he is the mediator of a <u>new covenant</u>, so that those who are called may <u>receive the promised eternal inheritance</u>…

Notice in this Hebrews passage below that the writer says that the promised land to Abraham was never the true promised land, but

Israel in Bible Prophecy

merely an earthly reference that looked forward to the true fulfillment of a heavenly land, a heavenly city.

> Hebrews 11:8–10, 15-16
>
> [8] By faith Abraham obeyed when he was called to go out to a place that he was to receive as <u>an inheritance</u>....[9] By faith he went to live in the <u>land of promise</u>, with Isaac and Jacob, <u>heirs with him of the same promise</u>. [10] For he was <u>looking forward to the city that has foundations, whose designer and builder is God</u>...[15] If they had been thinking of that land from which they had gone out, they would have had opportunity to return. [16] But as it is, <u>they desire a better country, that is, a heavenly one. Therefore God is not ashamed to be called their God, for he has prepared for them a city.</u>

That heavenly city of that eternal inheritance is the New Jerusalem, which is a metaphor for the New Covenant in Jesus Christ, the Messiah. The physical land of promise and the earthly city of God has been spiritually fulfilled in Christ.

> Hebrews 12:22–24
>
> [22] But you [Christians] have come to Mount Zion and <u>to the city of the living God, the heavenly Jerusalem</u>...and to Jesus, the mediator of a <u>new covenant</u>.

The inheritance of land in the Old Covenant has been transformed into an inheritance of international land without boundaries created by the "breaking down of the dividing wall" between Jew and Gentile. There can no longer be a geographical land that God is promising to his people because his people are international, from every tongue and nation. To affirm an earthly nationalistic plan of God is to reinstitute the Laws of separation between Jew and Gentile that Christ abolished. It is to break the "one man" back into two, which is what the Dispensationalist is trying to do by positing two "promises" of God, two "chosen peoples," two "children of Abraham."

> Ephesians 2:14-16
>
> [Christ] made both groups [Jew and Gentile] into one, and broke down the barrier of the dividing wall, 15 by abolishing in His

flesh the enmity, which is the Law of commandments contained in ordinances, that in Himself He might make the two into one new man...16 and might reconcile them both in one body to God through the cross, by it having put to death the enmity."

Galatians 3:28-29

There is neither Jew nor Greek, there is neither slave nor free man, there is neither male nor female; for you are all one in Christ Jesus. 29 And if you belong to Christ, then you are Abraham's offspring, heirs according to promise.

"Abolish" is a very powerful word. In the original Greek, it is the word, *katargeo;* which means "to render inoperative." Elsewhere in the Bible it is translated variously as "bring to an end," "nullify," "remove," and "render powerless." Abraham's descendants ("offspring"), the heirs of the promise, those who are "in Christ," are not separated from other nations. This is a very important key to understanding the nature of the New Covenant: Those **laws of separation between Jew and Gentile** have been abolished, "put to death," nullified, removed, rendered powerless!

And what is the biggest expression of separation between nations? LAND!!! In the Old Testament God was separating a national people unto Himself and giving them a separate piece of land to have among the nations. But with the New Covenant, that separation of land and people has been abolished. This is why Christianity claims there are no more Holy Wars in this New Covenant era; because the Holy Wars of Jehovah were tied directly to inheriting the geographical land in the Old Testament. Separation of Jew from Gentile. Since there is no more national distinction made by God, then he has no specific national or geographical interest in a parcel of land.

But this is not the entire picture. Actually, God does have a geographical interest in land. That is, He wants **all the earth** as the possession of the people of God, not a mere parcel of land in the Middle East! His meek ones shall inherit the earth! The kingdom of God is growing like a mustard seed into the biggest tree on earth (Matt 13:31-32). It is spreading like leaven through **all the earth**! (Matt

13:33). The cornerstone of Jesus Christ and his kingdom is, right now as you read this, growing to be a mountain that fills ***all the earth*** and crushes ***all other kingdoms*** (Dan 2:35) not a mere tract of sand and rock in the desert!

> Colossians 1:15
>
> And He is the image of the invisible God, the first-born of all creation....all things have been created by Him and for Him.

In this verse above, we see that Jesus is the first-born of all creation. Biblically, this is not a reference to Jesus being born or created, but rather an indication of status. That is, the first born son in the Old Testament economy was the primary inheritor of the father's estate. In fact, the first born had the birthright (Gen 43:33), The place of preeminence and power (Gen 49:3). He received a double portion of that inheritance (Deut 21:17). So the purpose of this Colossians verse is to indicate that Christ actually inherited all of creation, not merely a single parcel of it. The land promise is merely a metaphor for a creation-wide inheritance.

Here's the kicker: the Scriptures also say that Christians are joint heirs with Christ. Christians will inherit *all things* of that creation with him:

> Romans 8:17
>
> and if children, heirs also, heirs of God and fellow heirs with Christ.
>
> 1 Corinthians 3:21-22
>
> So then let no one boast in men. For all things belong to you, whether ... the world or life or death or things present or things to come; all things belong to you...

The serious error of Dispensationalism becomes crystal clear in this light of "inheritance": The proposal that God still maintains a promise of physical land to a nationally separated people of race is to deny the essence of the New Covenant. The land laws and separation laws are abolished in Christ; The promised land is now all the earth in Christ, not a desert patch. The Kingdom of God fulfills the land promise. God's chosen people are Jewish and Gentile believers in Messiah, not physically circumcised unbelieving Jews. The promotion of nationalistic racial interest is a negation of God's New Covenant interracial internationalism. In short, Dispensationalism is a kind of racism.

Related to this geographical promise are the terms, *Mount Zion* and *Jerusalem*. In Scripture, these terms are used, very often together, as symbolic references to the Kingdom of God, and the city of God, or God's reign. There are literally hundreds of such references, but here are just two:

> Zechariah 8:3
> "Thus says the LORD, 'I will return to Zion and will dwell in the midst of Jerusalem. Then Jerusalem will be called the City of Truth, and the mountain of the LORD of hosts will be called the Holy Mountain.'

> Micah 4:2
> And many nations will come and say, "Come and let us go up to the mountain of the LORD And to the house of the God of Jacob, That He may teach us about His ways And that we may walk in His paths." For from Zion will go forth the law, Even the word of the LORD from Jerusalem.

As you can readily see, I've chosen some specific verses that use Zion and Jerusalem in reference to Messiah, who of course, is Jesus Christ. Dispensationalists claim that these are all literal references to earthly Mount Zion and Jerusalem. But the New Testament defines the concepts of Zion and Jerusalem as ***heavenly***, or transcendent, which means they are terms that use literal locations as a metaphor for a more important spiritual idea. Sometimes they are references to the literal geographical sites in context, but in general, they are spiritual references to the Kingdom of God.

In Hebrews 12, the writer talks about Moses and the Old Covenant and how he received the Law on the mountain with blazing fire and God's glory. But then he shows that the Newer Covenant is not merely greater than the Older, but it is the true spiritual fulfillment of the "types and shadows" of the Old.

Hebrews 12:22–24

²² But you have come to Mount Zion and to the city of the living God, the heavenly Jerusalem, and to innumerable angels in festal gathering, ²³ and to the assembly of the firstborn who are enrolled in heaven, and to God, the judge of all, and to the spirits of the righteous made perfect, ²⁴ and to Jesus, the mediator of a new covenant.

Here, we see that the New Covenant *is* Mount Zion spoken of in the Old Covenant. Coming to Jesus *is* coming to the heavenly Jerusalem, the true spiritual reality that the Old Covenant types pointed to. There can be no physical earthly Jerusalem or Mount Zion that God is promising to do anything with, because His promise was fulfilled in Christ and His Kingdom, the heavenly (spiritual) Mount Zion and Jerusalem!

This is the theme of Hebrews: that the Old Covenant was a *physical* type or shadow of the spiritual reality which is in Jesus Christ:

Hebrews 8:5

[The priests of Old Covenant Law] serve a copy and shadow of heavenly things.

Hebrews 9:23

Therefore it was necessary for the copies of the things in the heavens to be cleansed with these [physical sacrifices], but the heavenly things themselves with better sacrifices than these. 24 For Christ did not enter a holy place made with hands, a mere copy of the true one, but into heaven itself, now to appear in the presence of God for us.

This heavenly Jerusalem corresponds to the "New Jerusalem that comes down out of heaven" in Revelation 21. The heavenly Jerusalem is the true Jerusalem, not the physical one. And the true, new Jerusalem is the New Covenant populated by believers in Christ, not mere circumcised genetic Israelites.

If there is any doubt left about this heavenly reality, the Apostle Paul, in a passage we saw earlier, emphasizes this true Jerusalem of promise as the Church of Christ consisting of believers in Christ:

Galatians 4:22–31

²² For it is written that Abraham had two sons, one by a slave woman and one by a free woman. ²³ But the son of the slave was born according to the flesh, while the son of the free woman was born through promise. ²⁴ Now this may be interpreted allegorically: these women are two covenants. One is from Mount Sinai, bearing children for slavery; she is Hagar. ²⁵ Now Hagar is Mount Sinai in Arabia; she corresponds to the present Jerusalem, for she is in slavery with her children. ²⁶ But the Jerusalem above is free, and she is our mother. ²⁷ For it is written, "Rejoice, O barren one who does not bear; break forth and cry aloud, you who are not in labor! For the children of the desolate one will be more than those of the one who has a husband." ²⁸ Now you, brothers, like Isaac, are children of promise. ²⁹ But just as at that time he who was born according to the flesh persecuted him who was born according to the Spirit, so also it is now. ³⁰ But what does the Scripture say? "Cast out the slave woman and her son, for the son of the slave woman shall not inherit with the son of the free woman." ³¹ So, brothers, we are not children of the slave but of the free woman.

Earthly Jerusalem is correlated with earthly Jews ("according to the flesh"). Those earthly unbelieving Jews are in slavery and **will not be heirs of God's promise** because **they are not** the children of promise. Believers in Christ are the free ones who will be heirs of God's promise to Abraham and Isaac. Mount Zion and Jerusalem are simply metaphors for the kingdom of God which is the Kingdom of God in the Church of Jesus Christ!

So, when the New Testament uses the word for "inheritance," it is talking about the land inheritance transformed into the Kingdom of God, which includes all creation that Christ will inherit, and we will inherit with him because we are "in Christ." Read these New Testament passages on spiritualized inheritance and you will understand why the authors stopped referring directly to a land promise, because the Kingdom of God is our inheritance, and that kingdom will consist of all the earth!

Ephesians 1:11–14

¹¹ In him we have obtained an inheritance... In him you also, when you heard the word of truth, the gospel of your salvation,

and believed in him, were sealed with the promised Holy Spirit, [14] who is the guarantee of our inheritance until we acquire possession of it.

Hebrews 9:15

[15] Therefore he is the mediator of a new covenant, so that those who are called may receive the promised eternal inheritance.

Matthew 5:5

[5] "Blessed are the meek, for they shall inherit the earth.

Acts 13:17–33

[17] [Stephen preaching to the Jews:] "The God of this people Israel chose our fathers…[19] And after destroying seven nations in the land of Canaan, he gave them their land as an inheritance… [32] And we bring you the good news that what God promised to the fathers, [33] this he has fulfilled to us their children by raising Jesus.'"

Ephesians 1:9–14

[9] according to his purpose, which he set forth in Christ [10] as a plan for the fullness of time, to unite all things in him, things in heaven and things on earth. [11] In him we have obtained an inheritance…[13] In him you also, when you heard the word of truth, the gospel of your salvation, and believed in him, were sealed with the promised Holy Spirit, [14] who is the guarantee of our inheritance until we acquire possession of it, to the praise of his glory.

Colossians 1:12–14

[12] giving thanks to the Father, who has qualified you to share in the inheritance of the saints in light. [13] He has delivered us from the domain of darkness and transferred us to the kingdom of his beloved Son, [14] in whom we have redemption, the forgiveness of sins.

Hebrews 11:8–16

[8] By faith Abraham obeyed when he was called to go out to a place that he was to receive as an inheritance. And he went out, not knowing where he was going. [9] By faith he went to live in the land of promise, as in a foreign land, living in tents with Isaac and Jacob, heirs with him of the same promise. [10] For he was looking forward to the city that has foundations, whose designer and builder is God… [14] For people who speak thus make it clear that they are seeking a homeland. [15] If they had been thinking of that land from which they had gone out, they would have had

opportunity to return. [16] But as it is, <u>they desire a better country, that is, a heavenly one. Therefore God is not ashamed to be called their God, for he has prepared for them a city.</u>

1 Peter 1:3–4

[3] According to his great mercy, he has caused us to be born again to a living hope through the resurrection of Jesus Christ from the dead, [4] <u>to an inheritance that is imperishable, undefiled, and unfading, kept in heaven for you.</u>

The New Testament has clearly transformed the notion of a physical land inheritance for Israel into a spiritual inheritance in Christ with an expansion of inheriting the entire earth. But Dispensationalists still hold onto Old Testament prophecies that promise that God will regather all the twelve earthly tribes of Israel from among the nations into the physical land of Israel. They believe that this regathering has yet to be fulfilled in our future. It has not happened yet in their scheme.

In the interest of keeping this narrative on target with the six-fold promise to Abraham, I have explained how this regathering is fulfilled in the New Testament in an added chapter at the end of this booklet, fittingly titled, "<u>The Regathering of Israel</u>."

6
Conditional Covenant

Genesis 17:9
[9] And God said to Abraham, "As for you, you shall keep my covenant, you and your offspring after you throughout their generations."

And now we come to the part in the covenant that Dispensationalists do not like, the conditional clause. On the one hand, these well-meaning Christians claim the everlasting nature of the covenant, but on the other hand they seem to miss it's expressed conditionality. Yes, the covenant is eternal, but to whom does it apply, the physical or the faithful? And what price does disobedience to the covenant bring? Jesus said it clearly in the parable of the vineyard:

Matthew 21:43
"Therefore I say to you, the kingdom of God will be taken away from you, and be given to a nation producing the fruit of it."

The Kingdom of God has been taken away from earthly Israel of Torah-observant Jews and given to the true spiritual Israel, the Church of believing Jews and Gentiles. The Kingdom of God is not tied to a geopolitical state inheriting physical land. In fact, in the parable, Jesus likens the ancient Jews to vinegrowers who reject the landowner and *forfeit all rights to the land*:

Matthew 21:33–41
[33] "Hear another parable. There was a master of a house who planted a vineyard and put a fence around it and dug a winepress in it and built a tower and leased it to tenants, and went into another country. [34] When the season for fruit drew near, he sent his servants to the tenants to get his fruit. [35] And the tenants took his servants and beat one, killed another, and stoned another. [36] Again he sent other servants, more than the

> first. And they did the same to them. ³⁷ Finally he sent his son to them, saying, 'They will respect my son.' ³⁸ But when the tenants saw the son, they said to themselves, 'This is the heir. Come, let us kill him and have his inheritance.' ³⁹ And they took him and threw him out of the vineyard and killed him. ⁴⁰ <u>When therefore the owner of the vineyard comes, what will he do to those tenants?" ⁴¹ They said to him, "He will put those wretches to a miserable death and let out the vineyard to other tenants who will give him the fruits in their seasons.</u>"

Christians have sometimes been falsely accused of anti-semitism because they point out the fact that the first century Jews are guilty of rejecting Messiah and are therefore condemned by God. They say that people who argue such things in the past used those beliefs to justify killing Jews because as "Christ killers."

This accusation of anti-Semitism is not only false, it is a libel and a slander. For one, it is a non-sequitir. Just because someone quotes the Bible as a rationalization for evil, does not mean that the Bible condones such evil. God himself has declared the first century Jews guilty of murdering Messiah, but he never commanded anyone to therefore go out and kill Jews because of it.

But even more obvious and more importantly, Dispensationalists seem to completely miss the point that it was Jesus himself who accused the first century Jews of being his murderers! And as we will see below, the apostles were also JEWS who condemned their own people for rejecting the Messiah, just as the ancient JEWISH prophets did. Those men of God were not anti-Semites, they were God's voice against his own people!

The point is that within the redemptive history of God, the physical Jews would so constantly reject him, even to the point of killing His Son, that He would take away His Kingdom from them to give to another "people" (involving the Gentiles) who were not originally His people, to be the inheritors of his Kingdom. Modern Jews are not judicially guilty of killing Christ, the first century Jews were guilty of this crime and therefore were judged by God in the destruction of the temple and holy city.

> Acts 7:51
>
> [Stephen:] "You men who are stiff-necked and uncircumcised in heart and ears are always resisting the Holy Spirit; you are doing just as your fathers did. 52 "Which one of the prophets did your fathers not persecute? And they killed those who had previously announced the coming of <u>the Righteous One, whose betrayers and murderers you have now become</u>.

> 1Thessalonians 2:14
>
> For you, brethren, ...also endured the same sufferings at the hands of your own countrymen, even as they {did} from the Jews, 15 who both killed the Lord Jesus and the prophets, and drove us out. They are not pleasing to God, but hostile to all men, 16 hindering us from speaking to the Gentiles that they might be saved; with the result that they always fill up the measure of their sins. But wrath has come upon them to the utmost.

As these verses show, the Jews have not obeyed the conditions of the Abrahamic covenant. They rejected Messiah so they are judged to the utmost by God. As a result, Gentiles are now becoming God's People.

The classic passage on the conditional nature of the covenant and how Gentiles now fulfill God's promises to Abraham is in Romans 11.

> Romans 11:1–7
>
> [1] I ask, then, has God rejected his people? By no means! For I myself am an Israelite, a descendant of Abraham, a member of the tribe of Benjamin. [2] God has not rejected his people whom he foreknew. Do you not know what the Scripture says of Elijah, how he appeals to God against Israel? [3] "Lord, they have killed your prophets, they have demolished your altars, and I alone am left, and they seek my life." [4] But what is God's reply to him? "I have kept for myself seven thousand men who have not bowed the knee to Baal." [5] So too at the present time there is a remnant, chosen by grace. [6] But if it is by grace, it is no longer on the basis of works; otherwise grace would no longer be grace. [7] What then? Israel failed to obtain what it was seeking. The elect obtained it, but the rest were hardened,

This passage is ***not*** saying that God has kept his promise to ***physical descendants*** of Israel. It is saying that God has kept his promise to the *remnant* of Israel who *are* true believers. Israel as a national entity did not obtain God's promises, but *chosen individuals* within that nation did. So God's promise was never to the physical many but to the faithful few. The physical many simply benefited from being outwardly aligned with the faithful few. The people who God *is not rejecting* in this passage are *not* physical Israel, but the remnant believers. The rest of the Jews are hardened and do not receive the promise because they are not true Israel.

> Romans 11:11–24
>
> [11] So I ask, did they stumble in order that they might fall? By no means! Rather through their trespass salvation has come to the Gentiles, so as to make Israel jealous. [12] Now if their trespass means riches for the world, and if their failure means riches for the Gentiles, how much more will their full inclusion mean! [13] Now I am speaking to you Gentiles. Inasmuch then as I am an apostle to the Gentiles, I magnify my ministry [14] in order somehow to make my fellow Jews jealous, and thus save some of them. [15] For if their rejection means the reconciliation of the world, what will their acceptance mean but life from the dead? [16] If the dough offered as firstfruits is holy, so is the whole lump, and if the root is holy, so are the branches. [17] But if some of the branches were broken off, and you, although a wild olive shoot, were grafted in among the others and now share in the nourishing root of the olive tree, [18] do not be arrogant toward the branches. If you are, remember it is not you who support the root, but the root that supports you. [19] Then you will say, "Branches were broken off so that I might be grafted in." [20] That is true. They were broken off because of their unbelief, but you stand fast through faith. So do not become proud, but fear. [21] For if God did not spare the natural branches, neither will he spare you. [22] Note then the kindness and the severity of God: severity toward those who have fallen, but God's kindness to you, provided you continue in his kindness. Otherwise you too will be cut off. [23] And even they, if they do not continue in their unbelief, will be grafted in, for God has the power to graft them in again. [24] For if you were cut from what is by nature a wild olive tree, and grafted, contrary to nature, into a cultivated olive tree, how much more will these, the natural branches, be grafted back into their own olive tree.

The key to understanding this passage is that the root of the tree is true spiritual Israel of Promise. And true Israel of Promise is not physical Israel, the land or the natural descendants. True Israel is simply the term for *God's people*—whoever they are. The natural branches represent physical descendants of Israel, while the wild olive branches represent Gentiles who believe. The conditional nature is emphasized here as Paul says that the physical earthly Jews were cut off because of their unbelief. **Faith is the root, not physical descent.**

Jews are rejected by God and cut off for disobeying the covenant. They are grafted back in **by faith**, just as Gentiles are grafted on **by faith**. A Jew gets saved, becomes God's chosen, the same way as a Gentile does: through faith in Christ, not physical descent. No physical or geopolitical Israel is here in mind. True Israel is the faithful, not the physical, the heavenly, not the earthly. Always was, always is, always will be.

The following conclusion of the passage has, in the eyes of some, reinforced that God has a special plan for physical Israel still:

> Romans 11:25–31
>
> [25] I do not want you to be unaware of this mystery, brothers: a partial hardening has come upon Israel, until the fullness of the Gentiles has come in. [26] And in this way all Israel will be saved, as it is written, "The Deliverer will come from Zion, he will banish ungodliness from Jacob"; [27] "and this will be my covenant with them when I take away their sins." [28] As regards the gospel, they are enemies for your sake. But as regards election, they are beloved for the sake of their forefathers. [29] For the gifts and the calling of God are irrevocable. [30] For just as you were at one time disobedient to God but now have received mercy because of their disobedience, [31] so they too have now been disobedient in order that by the mercy shown to you they also may now receive mercy.

Even if one takes this to be a reference to physical Israel, the context of the whole passage necessitates that God will show his electing mercy on the physical Jew the same way he does so on the Gentile -- through faith in Christ, not through an Old Covenant that is obsolete. God may very well cause a major revival of faith in the Jewish community in the future, but he will not do it apart from faith in Christ. He will not reinstitute ceremonial laws of Jewish separation and with it, a physical land promise and temple sacrifice, because these have already been fulfilled in Christ and there is no longer Jew or Gentile separation in Christ. Once the old is gone, it is gone forever. There is no returning.

> Hebrews 8:13
> When He said, "A new covenant," He has made the first obsolete."

If this Romans 11 passage means that God will save a mass of Jews in the future, he will do it through faith in Jesus Christ, not through a land grab which has been fulfilled already in Christ, or through returning to an obsolete understanding of physical land promise and national separation. To return to a nationalistic prejudice would be to negate the entire internationalism of the New Covenant. It would be a denial of the Gospel itself.

But in point of fact, I do not believe that this future revival of ethnic Israel is what Romans 11 is teaching. Paul is simply explaining the nature of the Gospel under the New Covenant.

Remember, earlier in this same passage, Paul differentiated between ethnic Israel and true Israel of faith by the concept of the remnant. He wrote that God *does not reject his people Israel*, but then he defines just exactly *who* those *people Israel* are, and they are not the ethnic descendants, but rather those *within ethnic Israel* who are true believers! The *remnant* are true Israel, the *remnant* are the ones who God does not reject. The *remnant* are the "elect" or "chosen" faithful. Genetic descent is the outward vehicle by which God creates the line for Messiah, but only the elect within that covenanted group obtain salvation by God's grace. *The rest are hardened* and do not receive it. Ethnic Jewishness gives no one status as the people of God.

So when Paul writes about the root and the branches with the branches being broken off because of unbelief, he is saying that faithless ethnic Israel rejects Messiah so that God can offer the Gentiles [nations] the same faith salvation that *true* faithful Israelites had.

Paul is referring to true Israel (of faith), both Jew and Gentile, when he writes, "and thus ['in this way'] all Israel will be saved." He is not saying that all ethnic Israel will be saved after God finishes saving all the Gentiles he was planning to save. Paul is saying that the New Covenant *is* the fullness of the nations, and that "in this way" both Jew and Gentile will be saved—by faith in Christ.

The Deliverer coming from Zion to remove ungodliness and taking away sins is the ***first*** coming of Jesus, not the second. The second coming is when Jesus brings judgment, not forgiveness.

So what does Paul mean when he says, "The gifts and calling of God are irrevocable"? The Dispensationalist argues that this means that God does not revoke his promises to Israel. And with that assertion, I would agree. BUT who is he referring to? All of ethnic Israel? May it never be! He explicitly speaks of "election." It is *the elect within ethnic Israel* whose calling and gifts are irrevocable. And those "elect" are the remnant of believers, not the physical descendants. Remember, that we pointed out earlier in this passage of Romans 11 that Paul claims the elect or chosen "remnant" are the true believers *within ethnic Israel*. The Greek word for "chosen" in that passage on the remnant is the same as the Greek word for "election" earlier in the same chapter.

So "partial hardening" does not refer to a *temporary time* of hardening, but to a *portion of the people* being hardened. This means that some of Israel ***did*** believe in Messiah. And these are the Israel that *are* saved [which includes believing Gentiles]. A partial hardening has happened to *ethnic* Israel so that God would bring the fullness of the nations (Gentiles), through faith, in with true Israel *of* faith. This is how God saves all Israel, all *true* Israel [both Jew and Gentile], as opposed to all ethnic Israel.

> Romans 9:6–8
>
> ⁶ For not all who are descended from Israel belong to Israel, ⁷ and not all are children of Abraham because they are his offspring, but "Through Isaac shall your offspring be named." ⁸ This means that it is not the children of the flesh who are the children of God, but the children of the promise are counted as offspring.

"All Israel" in Romans 11:26 is not a term referring to ethnic Israel, but a term that refers to *elect* Jew **and** Gentile believers in Christ. These elect remnant believers are the "all Israel" that are saved with the coming of the New Covenant in Jesus.

This difficult bouncing back and forth that Paul does in reference to ethnic Israel and spiritual Israel may have caused confusion over the years in biblical interpretation, but it is a common biblical technique. Jesus bounces back and forth in his definition of "offspring of Abraham."

> John 8:37–40
>
> ³⁷ I know that you are <u>offspring of Abraham</u>; yet you seek to kill me because my word finds no place in you. ³⁸ I speak of what I have seen with my Father, and you do what you have heard from your father." ³⁹ They answered him, "<u>Abraham is our father</u>." Jesus said to them, "If you were <u>Abraham's children</u>, you would be doing the works Abraham did."

First, Jesus says Abraham is their father, *then* he says Abraham is not their father, but Satan is. Jesus is not contradicting himself, he is merely making a distinction between ethnic descendency and true spiritual descendency. This kind of bouncing back and forth in definitions is exactly what Paul did in Romans 11. It may cause difficulty, but God never said it would be easy to discern the words of truth. We must study the Bible in its Near Eastern cultural context to show ourselves approved, not merely interpret things in our 21st century Western hyper-literalism. And if it's one thing that the New

Testament has made clear, it is that ethnic Israel as a whole did not obey the Old Covenant. They did not believe in the Messiah that the Old Covenant promised, so they forfeited their birthright as a whole. However, there was a remnant within that earthly whole that did obey and believe in Messiah. That Remnant received the promise to Abraham, because Abraham's children are those of faith, not flesh.

7
Circumcision

Genesis 17:10

¹⁰ This is my covenant, which you shall keep, between me and you and your offspring after you: Every male among you shall be circumcised.

In this conclusion of God's Promise to Abraham, we see that he seals the covenant with the act of circumcision. The thing to understand is that the physical act of circumcision was never the guarantee for physical Jews to inherit the promise. It was a physical sign of the ***spiritual circumcision*** that truly justifies a person.

In the New Testament, we are going to see that this was the point, but ironically, even in the Old Testament, God already stated that physical circumcision was not what determined a true Israelite, but spiritual circumcision.

Deuteronomy 30:6

⁶ And the LORD your <u>God will circumcise your heart</u> and the heart of your offspring, so that you will love the LORD your God with all your heart and with all your soul.

Jeremiah 4:4

⁴ <u>Circumcise yourselves</u> to the LORD; <u>remove the foreskin of your hearts,</u> O men of Judah and inhabitants of Jerusalem; lest my wrath go forth like fire, and burn with none to quench it, because of the evil of your deeds."

Jeremiah 9:25–26

²⁵ "Behold, the days are coming, declares the LORD, when I will punish all <u>those who are circumcised merely in the flesh—</u>
²⁶ ...for all these nations are uncircumcised, and all <u>the house of Israel are uncircumcised in heart.</u>"

We see in these Old Covenant passages that God already hints at the fact that to be disobedient to His covenant was to be uncircumcised of heart, which is the same as the uncircumcised heathen around them. In the New Covenant, this distinction is made more clearly by Paul as he tells us in Romans 3 that the circumcision God meant all along was spiritual circumcision of the heart. A "true Jew" is one who is circumcised of heart which means that a Gentile who believes is a true Jew but an earthly or ethnic Jew who does not believe is actually an uncircumcised heathen:

> Romans 2:28–29
>
> [28] For no one is a Jew who is merely one outwardly, nor is circumcision outward and physical. [29] But a Jew is one inwardly, and circumcision is a matter of the heart, by the Spirit, not by the letter. His praise is not from man but from God.

> Colossians 2:11
>
> [11] In him also you were circumcised with a circumcision made without hands, by putting off the body of the flesh, by the circumcision of Christ,

According to the New Covenant, the baptized believing Gentile is circumcised of heart, *which is what God had meant all along when he commanded circumcision*. It is the *believer* (Jew and Gentile) that is the descendant of Abraham who is circumcised of heart and therefore receives the sign and seal of the covenant eternally promised by God.

Paul furthers this argument in Romans 4 when he proves that circumcision of heart (faith) is the seal that God was referring to when he declared Abraham righteous. Physical circumcision was merely an outward sign of the inward reality.

> Romans 4:9–13
>
> [9] Is this blessing then only for the circumcised, or also for the uncircumcised? For we say that faith was counted to Abraham as righteousness. [10] How then was it counted to him? Was it before or after he had been circumcised? It was not after, but before he was circumcised. [11] He received the sign of circumcision as a seal of the righteousness that he had by faith while he was still uncircumcised. The purpose was to make

him the father of all who believe without being circumcised, so that righteousness would be counted to them as well, [12] and to make him the father of the circumcised who are not merely circumcised but who also walk in the footsteps of the faith that our father Abraham had before he was circumcised. [13] For the promise to Abraham and his offspring that he would be heir of the world did not come through the law but through the righteousness of faith.

Paul's' point is that physical circumcision is not *the deal*, it is *the seal* of a deal already made through faith. To be physically circumcised means that you should be spiritually circumcised of heart, but if you are not, then you are not circumcised in truth. The unbeliever's circumcision becomes uncircumcison.

So, you see how circumcision of heart actually fulfills God's original intentions? It is not that he made physical circumcision the key in the Old Covenant and then changed it with the New Covenant, it is that God **all along** meant circumcision of heart by the Spirit to be the true covenantal sign and seal, of which fleshly circumcision was only an outward picture. So the New Covenant does not *change* the meaning of circumcision, but rather *illuminates* its true meaning.

But Dispensationalists think that there are Scriptures that appear to support the notion that God still has a place in his plan for physical Israel. Romans 2:1-4 is one of them.

> Romans 3:1–4
>
> [1] Then what advantage has the Jew? Or what is the value of circumcision? [2] Much in every way. To begin with, the Jews were entrusted with the oracles of God. [3] What if some were unfaithful? Does their faithlessness nullify the faithfulness of God? [4] By no means!"

On first blush it may appear that God still holds earthly Israel as special in His eyes or that he remains "faithful" to earthly Israel. But in context, this is clearly *not* what He is talking about. This exclamation that God's faithfulness is not nullified by some unbelief is referring to God's faithfulness **to the remnant spiritual believers within earthly Israel**. In other words, God keeps his covenant **because of** the faithful few and *only to the* faithful few. Just because some do not believe does not mean that God will then withdraw from the faithful. God remains faithful to physically circumcised *believing* Jews, who are Abraham's descendants, along with believing Gentiles. This is not an exception for *earthly* Israel, this is a definition of *true* Israel, and true Israel includes both believing Gentiles and believing Jews.

Conclusion

As we have walked through each of the six elements of God's promise to Abraham and his offspring, we have seen that each and every one of them are not merely fulfilled spiritually in New Covenant faith, but that is what God had intended all along. 1) Abraham is a father of many nations through faith because the Gentiles are included through faith along with believing Jews; 2) The Children of Abraham have always been those who believe like Abraham did, not those who are born of flesh; 3) The everlasting covenant remains everlasting because it is fulfilled in Christ who is able to save those who draw near to him by faith, not because it is a deed to a piece of land in the Middle East; 4) The Promised Land is fulfilled in Jesus as we rest from our works in faith and inherit the earth. God does not deal with physical plots of land to separate his people from the nations because now, people from every nation are his people and God is international, respecting no land boundaries. All separation laws between Jew and Gentile have been abolished in Christ; 5) The covenant was conditional upon obedience, so Jesus took the inheritance away from those first century unbelieving Jews to open it up to Gentiles; 6) and God always intended spiritual circumcision as the sign and seal of the covenant, not mere physical circumcision. So faith accomplishes spiritual circumcision for believers, and unbelief operates as "uncircumcision" to physically circumcised Jews who reject Messiah.

Many Christians want modern day geopolitical Israel to still be God's Chosen People, as if they are still the center of God's prophetic plan for the future. They claim that God's Promise to Abraham is still in effect with physical Israel. But in attributing such a false identity to modern Israel, they are negating the Gospel of salvation by grace through faith in Jesus Christ, that applies all of Abraham's promise spiritually and truly to Christ and then to those who believe *in Christ*.

But wait, there's more!

8
The Temple

Another problem with the Dispensational obsession with physical earthly Israel is an equally disturbing obsession with the physical earthly temple in Jerusalem. Popular talk of the Red Heifer, the Ark of the Covenant and other political events surrounding Jerusalem and the temple mount, reveals a belief that the rebuilding of a physical temple in Jerusalem will presage the Second Coming of Christ, who will, in some hybrid fashion, reinstitute the laws of sacrifice that were abolished under the New Covenant. This bizarre retro scenario does not merely defy the imagination, it defies the Scriptures! If God were to reinstitute the temple with its sacrifices, he would be denying his own once-for-all sacrifice made by Christ (Heb 7:27, 9:12, 26).

Despite the fact that the New Testament nowhere says that the physical temple will be rebuilt, there is the promise of an eschatological temple in Ezekiel 40-48. Futurists (those who believe the last days are in our future) assume it is a physical temple, though the description of that temple is in a vision of obvious spiritual symbols, such as a trickle of living water, becoming an uncrossable river that flows out of the temple into the sea, turning the entire sea into freshwater (Ezke 47:1-12). Milton Terry, renowned expert on Biblical Apocalyptics concludes,

> Ezekiel's temple is no more explicable as a model of real architecture than are his cherubim and wheels possible in mechanics...this vision of restored and perfected temple,

service, and land symbolizes the perfected kingdom of God and his Messiah."[1]

In line with Terry's messianic interpretation of Ezekiel's eschatological temple, the Messiah is prophesied to build that temple:

> Zechariah 6:12–13 (ESV)
> [12] And say to him, 'Thus says the LORD of hosts, "Behold, the man whose name is the Branch: for he shall branch out from his place, and he shall build the temple of the LORD. [13] It is he who shall build the temple of the LORD and shall bear royal honor, and shall sit and rule on his throne." '

In the New Testament, Jesus is revealed as that "branch of Jesse" (Acts 13:22-23). So, Jesus, as Messiah, is the builder of the eschatological temple. But what kind of temple is it? The answer is to be found in the cornerstone.

The cornerstone of a temple is the "perfect" foundational stone upon which a temple is based. It is usually buried in the corner of the building, and all the rest of the structure is built upon it's perfect angles and measurements. The biblical prophecies describe that perfect cornerstone of the eschatological temple as Messiah himself:

> Isaiah 28:16 (ESV)
> [16] therefore thus says the Lord GOD, "Behold, I am the one who has laid as a foundation in Zion, a stone, a tested stone, a precious cornerstone, of a sure foundation: 'Whoever believes will not be in haste.'

Now, is that a spiritual metaphor or not? Obviously the text is not promising that the body of Messiah would literally be buried in the ground of a physical temple as its cornerstone. So if the very cornerstone of the eschatological temple is spiritual, then the entire temple, that is based upon it, would have to be a spiritual temple, not a physical one.

---

[1] Milton S. Terry, *Biblical Apocalyptics: A Study of the Most Notable Revelations of God and of Christ in the Canonical Scriptures* (New York; Cincinnati: Eaton & Mains; Curts & Jennings, 1898), 131.

Acts 4:11 (ESV)
¹¹ This <u>Jesus is the stone</u> that was rejected by you, the builders, <u>which has become the cornerstone</u>.

Isaiah 8:14 (ESV)
¹⁴ And <u>he will become a sanctuary and a stone of offense</u> and a rock of stumbling to both houses of Israel, a trap and a snare to the inhabitants of Jerusalem.

The Jews who rejected that cornerstone of the new temple would be judged when God came and destroyed their physical temple to replace it with the spiritual one in AD 70 (Matt 21:40-43). The simple biblical fact is: the new temple of God in the New Covenant era is not an earthly temple built with hands, but a heavenly one built by the Spirit.

But don't take my word for it, the apostles who wrote the Scriptures also told us that the temple was transformed into the spiritual reality of Jesus Christ himself. Jesus is the New Temple.

John 1:14
¹⁴ And the Word became flesh and dwelt [tabernacled] among us, and we have seen his glory, glory as of the only Son from the Father, full of grace and truth.

In this passage, Jesus is described using the term for tabernacle, which was the precursor to the temple. As argued above, the "New Jerusalem" is a spiritual metaphor for the New Covenant (Heb 12:22–24; Gal 4:22–31). In that New Covenant "city," there is no physical stone temple, because Jesus is God's true and spiritual temple:

Revelation 21:22
²² And I saw no temple in the city [New Jerusalem], for its temple is the Lord God the Almighty and the Lamb.

This revelation of the New Jerusalem in Revelation is not a future reality, but a present one. New Jerusalem is the New Covenant (Heb 12:22) described as a spiritual building.

The apostle Paul makes that spiritual temple connection crystal clear when he speaks of the new holy temple of God, "being built on the foundation of the apostles and prophets, Christ Jesus himself being the cornerstone" (Eph 2:20).

> Ephesians 2:19–22
>
> [19] So then you are no longer strangers and aliens, but you are fellow citizens with the saints and members of the household of God, [20] built on the foundation of the apostles and prophets, Christ Jesus himself being the cornerstone, [21] <u>in whom the whole structure, being joined together, grows into a holy temple in the Lord.</u> [22] <u>In him you also are being built together into a dwelling place for God by the Spirit.</u>

The new temple of God here is not a physical one rebuilt with stone, but a spiritual house consisting of the body of Christ. This is not mere "spiritualizing," as if it doesn't have any tangible reality. No, the Church of Jesus Christ is a real presence of people in this world, and it is the true presence of Jesus Christ as well, not a mere metaphor. In the Bible, "spiritualization" does not mean something is any less real, in fact, it is in some ways *more* real. The Body of Christ as God's "spiritual" temple is a very real and tangible presence of God on the earth.

Peter affirms this same notion of the body of Christ being God's "spiritual" holy temple in this new covenant.

> 1 Peter 2:4–6
>
> [4] As you come to him, a living stone rejected by men but in the sight of God chosen and precious, [5] <u>you yourselves like living stones are being built up as a spiritual house</u>, to be a holy priesthood, to offer spiritual sacrifices acceptable to God through Jesus Christ. [6] For it stands in Scripture: "Behold, I am laying in Zion a stone, a cornerstone chosen and precious, and whoever believes in him will not be put to shame."

> 2 Corinthians 6:16
>
> [16] For <u>we are the temple of the living God</u>; as God said, "I will make my dwelling among them and walk among them, and I will be their God, and they shall be my people.

Scholar Richard Bauckham points out that during the Jerusalem council of Acts 15, James describes an eschatological temple that God prophesies to rebuild as being the body of Christ, consisting of believing Gentiles added to believing Jews.

> Acts 15:13–17
>
> [13] After they finished speaking, James replied, "Brothers, listen to me. [14] Simeon has related how God first visited the Gentiles, to take from them a people for his name. [15] And with this the words of the prophets agree, just as it is written, [16] " 'After this **I will return, and I will rebuild the tent ["dwelling"] of David that has fallen; I will rebuild its ruins, and I will restore it**, [17] that **the remnant** of mankind may seek the Lord, and all the Gentiles who are called by my name, says the Lord, who makes these things
>
> "The interpretation takes 'the dwelling of David' to be the eschatological temple which God will build, as the place of his eschatological presence, in the messianic age when Davidic rule is restored to Israel. He will build this new temple so that all the Gentile nations may seek his presence there."[2]

So there is a rebuilt temple after all. And God is rebuilding that temple right now. But it is a heavenly temple, with Christians as living stones (1Pet 2:5)—as opposed to dead rocks—and apostles and prophets as foundation and pillars (Eph 2:20), and Jesus Christ as the cornerstone (1Cor 3:11; Eph 2:20). Jesus Christ is the new temple and high priest of that true heavenly temple/tabernacle (Heb 9:11, 23-24)!

Not only that, but the Church is also the holy priesthood that ministers the atonement of God to the world through the Gospel. There is no longer a physical Jewish priesthood before God. In fact, God calls the Church his *chosen race, a holy nation, people for his own possession*, all terms that were applied to Israel in the Old Covenant.

> 1 Peter 2:9–10
>
> [9] But you are a <u>chosen race, a royal priesthood, a holy nation, a people for his own possession</u>, that you may proclaim the excellencies of him who called you out of darkness into his

---

[2] Richard Bauckham, "James and the Jerusalem Church," in *The Book of Acts in Its First Century Setting: The Book of Acts in Its Palestinian Setting*, ed. Richard Bauckham and Bruce W. Winter, vol. 4 (Grand Rapids, MI; Carlisle, Cumbria: William B. Eerdmans Publishing Company; The Paternoster Press, 1995), 453–454.

marvelous light. [10] Once you were not a people, but now <u>you are God's people</u>; once you had not received mercy, but now you have received mercy.

The physical temple of stone in Jerusalem was a weak physical shadow of the true heavenly temple explained in Hebrews 8 through 10. It would be sacrilege to suggest that God would return to an inferior physical shadow after the perfect spiritual reality has come. Christ has made his once for all sacrifice. It would be an abomination and denial of the New Covenant to return to the Old Testament priesthood and sacrifices. The book of Hebrews calls that return to the Old "apostasy" (Heb 6:4-8).

The total desolation of the earthly temple in AD 70 was God's way of saying the last days of the Old Covenant had arrived, the consummation of the ages was here (Heb 9:26), the Old Covenant and its priesthood and sacrificial system was obsolete (Heb 8:13). The New Heavenly Jerusalem and Zion has come out of heaven and replaced the old physical Jerusalem and Zion (Heb 12:22-24; Rev 21).

If the current geopolitical nation of Israel ever does rebuild the temple, it will be a spiritually dead carcass of an obsolete letter of death, rather than a living reminder of a spiritually alive reality (1 Cor 3). Though I suspect there is a reason why God has never let the earthly temple be rebuilt. It is his way of historically verifying that the Old Covenant is obsolete and can never be reinstituted.

Let the writer of Hebrews have the final word on the temporary nature of the earthly physical tabernacle/temple embodying the Old Covenant, versus the permanent eternal nature of the heavenly temple embodying the New Covenant.

Hebrews 8:1–7

[1] Now the point in what we are saying is this: we have such a high priest, one who is seated at the right hand of the throne of the Majesty in heaven, [2] a minister in the holy places, in the true tent that the Lord set up, not man... [6] But as it is, Christ has obtained a ministry that is as much more excellent than the old as the covenant he mediates is better, since it is enacted on

better promises. ⁷ For if that first covenant had been faultless, there would have been no occasion to look for a second.

The author of Hebrews then concludes that this "second" covenant or heavenly temple is not historically consummated until the physical temple is destroyed. "The Holy Spirit *is* signifying this, that the way into the holy place has not yet been disclosed while the outer tabernacle is still standing" (Heb 9:8 NASB95).

The book of Hebrews was written before the temple was destroyed in AD 70. The writer and his Christian audience knew the desolation was coming because Jesus had foretold it (Matt 23:37-24:1). They were in a transition period between covenants. The New Covenant had been spiritually inaugurated at Christ's death, resurrection and ascension. But the earthly elements of the Old Covenant were still standing. The Old Covenant was becoming obsolete as the New Covenant was taking its place. The Old Covenant was about to finally and fully vanish away—when the earthly incarnation of that Old Covenant was destroyed: the holy city and temple.

> Hebrews 8:13
> ¹³ In speaking of a new covenant, he makes the first one obsolete. And what is becoming obsolete and growing old is ready to vanish away.

Hebrews was written in a transition period. In an earthly sense, the New Covenant had been inaugurated, but not consummated until the Old Covenant had been completely done away by the destruction of the earthly incarnation of that Old Covenant. When the Roman armies destroyed the earthly city of Jerusalem and its temple, that marked God historically consummating the New Covenant that he had previously spiritually inaugurated. I explain this in much more detail in my book <u>End Times Bible Prophecy: It's Not What They Told You.</u>

9
Blessing and Cursing

So none of the promises to Abraham can possibly refer to physical Israel in the current national climate because it is all fulfilled in Christ and the New Covenant. The physical nation of Israel is not God's Chosen People, the church of Jesus Christ is the "Israel of God (Gal 6:16), God's Chosen People from every nation on earth. The promise that Dispensationalists use from the Old Testament to refer to blessing and cursing of physical Israel is actually a promise related to *true spiritual* Israel, the Church of God.

> Genesis 12:3
> "I will bless those who bless you, And the one who curses you I will curse. And in you all the families of the earth shall be blessed."

This is part of the same Promise God made to Abraham. The phrase "in you all the families of the earth shall be blessed" is a connective phrase to the original promise made to Abraham. We have already shown how this has been fulfilled in the New Testament Church of Jesus Christ, so the blessing and cursing is not upon those who bless and curse physical Israel, but upon those who bless and curse spiritual Israel, the Body of Christ.

America was founded on Christianity. As it dismantles its Christian roots, it departs from this blessing, and so it will lose God's favor. America is not blessed because it has blessed Israel. Israel is blessed because it has blessed America, at one time, a country based on a Christian worldview. This is not to say that America is the Promised Land or any such nonsense. It is simply saying that America was blessed because it reverenced God as the Church followed Christ and grew in its midst (remember the "Remnant"?). America was blessed long before the modern state of Israel was founded in 1948. Of course, as America departs from its Christian roots, as the last vestiges of Christianity in our justice, political, social and economic systems disappear, we will learn what it is like to lose God's favor. May God bless America because America has blessed the Lord and His Church. But may God have mercy on us as we depart from His ways.

10
The Regathering of Israel

One of the reasons why Dispensationalists believe that the promise of a physical land to earthly Israel remains intact is the repeated prediction by most all of the Old Testament prophets of a "regathering" of the twelve tribes of Israel back to the Land by Messiah. It's also called "the restoration of Israel." Though earthly Israel had been exiled and scattered to the ends of the earth (Diaspora) because of their disobedience to Yahweh, nevertheless, he would one day bring them all back into the land promised to their forefather, Abraham. The "lost ten tribes" of the Assyrian exile, collectively known as Israel (the northern kingdom) now in the Diaspora all over the earth, would one day come back and be united with Judah (the southern kingdom, including Benjamin). These returning exiles will be called "the remnant," and Messiah will be their shepherd and king.

Here are a few of the many passages reiterating this important prophecy:

Ezekiel 36:24
I will take you from the nations and gather you from all the countries and bring you into your own land.

Amos 9:9–15
[9] "For behold, I will command, and shake the house of Israel among all the nations as one shakes with a sieve...[14] I will restore the fortunes of my people Israel, and they shall rebuild the ruined cities and inhabit them;...[15] I will plant them on their land, and they shall never again be uprooted.

Micah 2:12
I will surely assemble all of you, O Jacob; I will gather the remnant of Israel; I will set them together like sheep in a fold.

Isaiah 11:10–12

> In that day the Lord will extend his hand yet a second time to recover the remnant that remains of his people, from Assyria, from Egypt, from Pathros, from Cush, from Elam, from Shinar, from Hamath, and from the coastlands of the sea. [12] He will raise a signal for the nations and will assemble the banished of Israel, and gather the dispersed of Judah from the four corners of the earth.

This regathering of the remnant of Israel is so often repeated in the Old Testament, it is surely one of the most significant themes of God's promises to His people. Because the Dispensationalist prioritizes Old Covenant earthly Israel over the New Covenant spiritual Israel (the Church of Jew and Gentile), he thinks this is an event that has yet to happen in our future. Sure, he says, some Jews believed in Jesus in the first century; sure, Israel became a modern state in 1948, with Jews coming back from amongst "all the nations." But, as a whole, they have yet to embrace Jesus the Messiah, so that regathering and restoration must be in our future—all according to their theology.

This interpretation is a spiritually dangerous one for Christians to have. Why? Because it completely ignores the New Covenant, and in some ways denies it. It operates as if Jesus did not fulfill the very prophecies that the New Testament said he did.

A closer look at the full context of each of these passages reveals several interwoven elements of the prophecy that New Testament apostles and writers claim are fulfilled in the New Covenant: 1) The regathering of the twelve tribes would occur with the coming of Messiah; 2) It would be a new covenant; 3) It would involve a remnant of true believers out of the rest of unbelieving Israel; 4) It would also include Gentiles along with Jews; and 5) God would dwell in their midst. All these elements above constitute the definition of the New Covenant that Jesus the Messiah accomplished in his death, resurrection, ascension and establishment of his kingdom. To deny that God has fulfilled these promises, is tantamount to denying the Gospel. It is no wonder that some Christian Zionists are telling Christians to not try to convert unbelieving Jews to Messiah Jesus. Why should we, they reason, since earthly Jews are still God's people and they will eventually believe in Jesus later in their end times scheme? This is madness based on a bizarre hermeneutic of hyperliteralism that misconstrues every one of the five elements of the regathering *against* the Gospel they are supposed to believe upon.

Let's take a closer look at just a few of these passages of the regathering and see how the New Testament says they are fulfilled in the first century inauguration of the New Covenant Gospel.

Acts and the Beginning of the Restoration

In Acts 2, we read about the first explosion of the Gospel with the first baptism of the Holy Spirit. It was the thing that Jesus had told them to wait for, which would launch them into all the world with the Good News (Acts 1:4). Pentecost would be the historical inauguration of the heavenly New Covenant achieved by the death, resurrection and ascension of Christ. It would be the pouring out of God's Spirit upon his people (Isa 32:12-19; 44:5; Ezek 36:25-28; 37:14).

The disciples asked Jesus if this was the time of the restoration of Israel (1:6), the very thing we have been discussing in this work. Jesus told them that the restoration of Israel would begin occurring when the Holy Spirit came upon them, but they were not to worry themselves with the timing (1:8).

And what was the restoration, but the pouring out of God's Spirit and the regathering of Jews from all over the known earth in a spiritual metaphorical resurrection? (Ezek 37). So when the disciples were baptized with the Spirit at Pentecost and began to speak in foreign tongues, that was the fulfillment of God's pouring out of his Spirit. Pouring is a form of baptizing (Heb 9:10, 13, 19, 21). But it was also the beginning of the regathering of Jews because "there were dwelling in Jerusalem Jews, devout men from every nation under heaven" (Acts 2:5). The list of nations that are described (Acts 2:9-11) just happens to be a representative sampling of the seventy nations of Genesis 10. To the ancient Jew, those seventy were "all the nations" to which the Jews were scattered (Amos 9:9). According to the apostle Luke, Pentecost of AD 30 was transformed into the beginning of the gathering of Jews from all the nations.

And that gathering of Jews included the Gentiles. It was a gathering of two bodies into one that was occurring all throughout the book of Acts. Notice these passages that say that the evangelism of Acts is the very fulfillment of the promise to gather the Gentiles with the Jews as his people:

> Acts 15:13–19 (ESV)
> [13] After they finished speaking, James replied, "Brothers, listen to me. [14] Simeon has related how <u>God first visited the Gentiles, to take from them a people for his name.</u> [15] <u>And with this the words of the prophets agree</u>, just as it is written.

> Acts 26:23 (ESV)
> [Paul:] [23] that the Christ must suffer and that, by being the first to rise from the dead, <u>he would proclaim light both to our people and to the Gentiles.</u>"

The "ingathering" was based upon the unity of belief in Jesus as Messiah. Isaiah had prophesied that when Messiah first came (the branch of Jesse), *in that very day*, the Lord would "recover the remnant that remains of his people," from all the nations. "In that day," the root of Jesse would be "raised (resurrected) as a signal for the nations," and would "assemble the banished of Israel and gather the dispersed of Judah from the four corners of the earth" (Isa 11:1-2, 10-12). According to the prophecy, the gathering of the remnant and the Gentiles would occur at the *first coming* of Messiah, when Jesus was resurrected, not the second coming. *In that day* of Messiah's arrival and resurrection (his raising as a signal), he would draw both the remnant of Israel as well as Gentile believers. This will not start in our future, it already started in the book of Acts! Paul likened that raising of the signal to Christ's resurrection, and confirmed this Isaianic promise as already being fulfilled *during his ministry*:

> Romans 15:8–9, 12
>
> [8] For I tell you that <u>Christ became a servant</u> to the circumcised to show God's truthfulness, <u>in order to confirm the promises given to the patriarchs,</u> [9] and in order that the Gentiles might glorify God for his mercy…[12] And again <u>Isaiah says, "The root of Jesse will come, even he who arises to rule the Gentiles; in him will the Gentiles hope.</u>

What were the promises given to the patriarchs that Paul says were confirmed ("verified") in Christ's resurrection? All of them, including the regathering (Acts 3:24; 32; 15:13-15; 24:24; 26:6). In fact, most of the prophecies about the regathering of Israel almost always add the inclusion of Gentiles as a simultaneous event (See more below). But the point is that the book of Romans says explicitly that the Isaianic prophecy about the gathering of the remnant along with the Gentiles was already being fulfilled *in his own day*. This is not an eschatological system demanding something must be fulfilled in the future, this is the New Testament itself saying the prophecy was fulfilled in the first century, *in that day*.

One of the ways that Dispensationalists seek to deny the fulfillment of the regathering is to suggest that the inclusion of the Gentiles has been fulfilled in Christ, but the gathering of Israel has not yet been fulfilled. They argue that "confirmation" of promises to the patriarchs is not the same as "fulfillment." God only verified the promises to Israel, not fulfilled them. They see this split because they do not see an earthly nation called Israel regathered into the land in the way that they expect it to be. But their problem is that, as we have seen, the gathering of the Jews was simultaneous with the gathering of the Gentiles. If we return to Acts 2, the holy Scripture says again that both the gathering *and* Gentile inclusion were being fulfilled *in their day*.

They Were in the Last Days *of the Old Covenant*

Back to Pentecost. Peter then preaches a sermon about how they were in the last days as Joel described, a time when the "Day of the Lord" was coming for Israel. That Day of the Lord was the destruction of Jerusalem and the temple in AD 70. This has to be the case because Peter clearly states that the "last days" and "Day of the Lord" of Joel were being fulfilled in AD 30, not in a distant future (Acts 2:16. See my book *End Times Bible Prophecy* for the details on this). There could be no more explicit claim of Joel 2 being fulfilled in their day than Peter saying, "This is what was uttered through the prophet Joel." (Acts 2:16). *This is* what was uttered. Not, "this will be," or "this is like what will be." ***This is*** what was uttered.

Then he describes Joel's words about God's spirit poured out, wonders in the heavens, and the Day of the Lord. Some modern interpreters say that only the Spirit outpouring was fulfilled. But Peter says all of it was being fulfilled, and they were about to see the Day of the Lord. Peter does not quote the entire prophecy. Not because he is only quoting what was fulfilled but because they were only at the beginning of the fulfillment of that entire prophecy, which was a seamless and integrated whole. And guess what? If you look at that Joel prophecy in more detail, it includes this little gem right after Peter's quoted section:

> Joel 3:1
> "For behold, in those days and at that time, when I restore the fortunes of Judah and Jerusalem.

So Peter quotes Joel's prophecy that links the restoration to the last days and the Spirit outpouring, that Peter said was being fulfilled in their very midst, leading to the Day of the Lord (the destruction of Jerusalem and the temple). Christians tend to assume that the "Day of the Lord" is a reference to a universal end of time judgment. But in the Bible, it is not. In the Bible, it is used of local judgments by God on nations, peoples or cities (Zeph 1:7-15; Isa 13:6-19). The Day of the Lord Peter refers to is not the worldwide universal judgment, but the localized national and city judgment of God upon Jerusalem that Jesus had also prophesied (Matt 23:37-24:2; 21:37-45; 22:1-9; Luke 19:41-44).

The apostles knew they were in the last days in the first century. They said so without ambiguity (Heb 1:1; 9:26; 1Pet 1:20; 4:7; 1Cor 10:11; 1Jn 2:18; 4:3). The New Testament explicitly states that the first century were the last days. Therefore, they could not have been the last days of the whole world, but the last days of the Old Covenant.[1]

And part of those last days of the Old Covenant was the regathering of Israel at the coming of Messiah. When Messiah comes the first time (not the second time), he will regather Israel and be a light to the nations. Isaiah makes that link in chapter 49:

> Isaiah 49:6–8
>
> 6 he says: "It is too light a thing that you should be my servant to raise up the tribes of Jacob and to bring back the preserved of Israel; I will make you as a light for the nations... Thus says the LORD: "In a time of favor I have answered you; in a day of salvation I have helped you; I will keep you and give you as a covenant to the people, to establish the land, to apportion the desolate heritage.

First, notice that bringing back the preserved of Israel was about making them as a light for the nations or Gentiles. That phrase was a messianic one. When the old man Simeon, filled with the Holy Spirit saw the infant Jesus in the temple, he quoted Isaiah 49:

> Luke 2:30–32
>
> 30 for my eyes have seen your salvation 31 that you have prepared in the presence of all peoples, 32 a light for revelation to the Gentiles, and for glory to your people Israel."

When the Jews had rejected the apostle Paul's preaching of the Gospel, he concluded that Isaiah 49 was being fulfilled in his ministry of the Gospel to the Gentiles:

---

[1] See "Chapter 9: End of the Age/Last Days," Brian Godawa, *End Times Bible Prophecy: It's Not What They Told You* (Embedded Pictures, 2017), 70-80.

Israel in Bible Prophecy

> Acts 13:46–47
> [46] And Paul and Barnabas spoke out boldly, saying, "It was necessary that the word of God be spoken first to you. Since you thrust it aside and judge yourselves unworthy of eternal life, behold, we are turning to the Gentiles. [47] <u>For so the Lord has commanded us, saying, " 'I have made you a light for the Gentiles, that you may bring salvation to the ends of the earth.' "</u>

So the New Testament says that Isaiah 49:6-8 was being fulfilled in the first century coming of Messiah. But is that only one half of the prophecy fulfilled? The Acts 13 passage only mentions the Gentile inclusion, not the regathering of Israel. Dispensationalists believe that Jesus is the light to the Gentiles now, but that the time of gathering of Israel, her time of salvation, is yet in our future. There's only one problem: Paul disagrees with them. Paul writes to the Corinthians and quotes Isaiah 49 again by saying that Israel's time of salvation (another phrase for the regathering) was happening in his day!

> 2 Corinthians 6:1–2
> [1] Working together with him, then, we appeal to you not to receive the grace of God in vain. [2] For he says, "In a favorable time I listened to you, and in a day of salvation I have helped you." <u>Behold, now is the favorable time; behold, now is the day of salvation.</u>

If we go back to the Isaiah passage that Paul is quoting, we see that the "favorable time of salvation" includes the regathering to the Land!

> Isaiah 49:8 (NASB95)
> Thus says the LORD, "In <u>a favorable time</u> I have answered You, And in <u>a day of salvation</u> I have helped You; And I will keep You and give You for a covenant of the people, <u>To restore the land, to make them inherit the desolate heritages;</u>

Restoring the land and inheriting the desolate heritages is precisely the fulfillment of God's Promise to restore them to the Land of their inheritance. But the New Testament authors are claiming that the restoration is a spiritual return in Messiah, not a physical return to a physical land.

We need to put aside our own modern biased assumptions of how fulfillment operates and seek to understand what the meaning of fulfillment is to the New Testament apostles and prophets. If they say it was fulfilled, then we need to adjust our definition of fulfillment to their definition of fulfillment. And all too often the hyperliteralism of modern Dispensationalism interprets prophecies in a literal manner, when they are clearly poetic metaphors or spiritual interpretations of the ancient Hebrew.

But as we continue through Acts 2, we see that poetic and spiritual fulfillment even more so.

The Throne of David

After saying that the last days were being fulfilled in their midst, Peter describes Jesus as being seated on the throne of David at his resurrection and subsequent ascension to God's right hand.

> Acts 2:30–33
>
> [30] Being therefore a prophet, and knowing that God had sworn with an oath to him that he would <u>set one of his descendants on his throne</u>, [31] he foresaw and <u>spoke about the resurrection of the Christ</u>, that he was not abandoned to Hades, nor did his flesh see corruption. [32] This Jesus God raised up, and of that we all are witnesses. [33] <u>Being therefore exalted at the right hand of God</u>.

What is important about this fulfillment is that the New Testament apostle said that Jesus was enthroned as the Son of David *at his resurrection and ascension*, not in a future day from ours. This is crucial because the Old Testament prophecies said that *the Son of David would be enthroned at the time of the gathering of the remnant*!

> Ezekiel 37:7–14
>
> Behold, <u>I will take the people of Israel from the nations</u> among which they have gone, and will gather them from all around, and bring them to their own land... [24] "<u>My servant David shall be king over them, and they shall all have one shepherd</u>.

Ezekiel 34:11–24

[11] "For thus says the Lord GOD: [12] As a shepherd seeks out his flock when he is among his sheep that have been scattered, so will I seek out my sheep, and <u>I will rescue them from all places where they have been scattered</u>. [13] And I will bring them out from the peoples and <u>gather them from the countries, and will bring them into their own land</u>...[23] And I will <u>set up over them one shepherd, my servant David</u>, and he shall feed them: he shall feed them and be their shepherd.

The reference here to David is obviously a spiritual symbol of Messiah. David will not literally raise from the dead, but rather, a Son of David, that is, one from his lineage would be enthroned as a Davidic figure of salvation: Messiah! Jesus will not reign from an earthly throne of David in the future, he is already reigning right now on David's throne in heaven! (Eph 1:20-23).

Hyperliteralists want to believe that Jesus will sit on an earthly throne of David in the geographical earthly city of Jerusalem in our future. But Peter, the apostle of God, declares, with God's own authority, that *Jesus was seated on David's throne at his ascension.* And Ezekiel says that that enthronement occurs at the time of the regathering of Israel and the inclusion of the Gentiles into one people with one shepherd and king (Jeremiah repeats the same gathering of the remnant at the kingship of Messiah in Jer 23:3-6).

Again, this making of the two peoples, Jew and Gentile, into one people has already been declared by Jesus and his apostles to have been fulfilled. Jesus surely alludes to this Ezekiel prophecy when he refers to Gentiles as "sheep not of the fold" of Israel that he would make one with the Jews:

John 10:16

[16] And I have other sheep that are not of this fold. I must bring them also, and they will listen to my voice. So there will be one flock, one shepherd.

Jesus claimed that he was the fulfillment of Ezekiel's shepherd bringing Jew and Gentile into one flock. But more importantly, the apostle Paul writes that this making of Gentiles one with Jews (through faith – Ephesians 2:8) already occurred through Christ's death and resurrection. Ezekiel's prophecy about the gathering of Jews and Gentiles from all the nations into the one fold of God's sheep is the Gospel of Jesus Christ! Ephesians says that regathering is fulfilled in the Church of Jesus Christ: Jew and Gentile, one in Christ.

> Ephesians 2:13–15
>
> [13] But now in Christ Jesus <u>you [Gentiles] who once were far off have been brought near by the blood of Christ</u>. [14] For he himself is our peace, who has <u>made us both one</u> and has broken down in his flesh the dividing wall of hostility [15] by abolishing the law of commandments expressed in ordinances, that <u>he might create in himself one new man in place of the two, so making peace</u>.

To finish up my brief look at the book of Acts, let's look at another sermon by Peter in Acts 15. In this case, he is speaking to fellow Christians who were struggling with Judaizers who were demanding Gentiles obey the laws of Moses in order to be God's people. The apostle James then quotes from the prophet Amos to justify the Gentile inclusion:

> Acts 15:13–19
>
> [13] James replied, "Brothers, listen to me. [14] Simeon has related how God first visited the Gentiles, to take from them a people for his name. [15] <u>And with this the words of the prophets agree, just as it is written,</u> [16] "'After this I will return, and I will rebuild the tent of David that has fallen; I will rebuild its ruins, and I will restore it, [17] that the remnant of mankind may seek the Lord, and all the Gentiles who are called by my name, says the Lord, who makes these things [18] known from of old.' [19] Therefore my judgment is that we should not trouble those of the Gentiles who turn to God,

The rebuilding of the tent or tabernacle of David is another poetic metaphor of the regathering of Israel by Messiah (Jesus). But notice how that metaphor is tied inextricably to the inclusion of the Gentiles? The two are always together. God will draw remnant Israel from the nations *and* unite them with the Gentile believers. James does not say that the inclusion of the Gentiles is fulfilled, but the rebuilding of David's tabernacle is not fulfilled. He quotes *the whole of the unit as fulfilled*. He says explicitly that God taking Gentiles as a people for his name was the fulfillment of the restoration of Israel and the remnant, which together is the rebuilding of the Davidic reign of Messiah.

Here is the original prophecy from Amos that James quoted. Notice how the regathering of Israel from the nations and its restoration is part of a unified whole including the Gentiles.

> Amos 9:9–15
>
> [9] "For behold, I will command, and <u>shake the house of Israel among all the nations</u> as one shakes with a sieve…[11] "In that day I will <u>raise up the booth of David that is fallen</u> and repair its breaches, and <u>raise up its ruins and rebuild it</u> as in the days of old, [12] <u>that they may possess the remnant of Edom and all the nations who are called by my name</u>,"… [14] I will <u>restore the fortunes of my people Israel</u>, and they shall rebuild the ruined cities and inhabit them;…[15] I will <u>plant them on their land</u>, and they <u>shall never again be uprooted out of the land</u> that I have given them," says the LORD your God.

So, why does the New Testament say nothing about the Jews in a physical land? Because the Gospel of the Kingdom of God has transformed the physical land of Israel into all the earth, as we explained in chapter 5, and because the "desire" of Abraham and the prophets for a homeland was revealed in the New Testament to be fulfilled in a heavenly land, city and temple, not physical ones.

Notice in this first passage of Hebrews 11 how the physical land of promise is described as Abraham's "inheritance."

> Hebrews 11:8–10
>
> [8] By faith Abraham obeyed when he was called to go out to a place that he was to <u>receive as an inheritance</u>. And he went out, not knowing where he was going. [9] By faith he went to live in the <u>land of promise</u>, as in a foreign land, living in tents with Isaac and Jacob, <u>heirs with him of the same promise</u>. [10] For he was looking forward to <u>the city that has foundations, whose designer and builder is God</u>.

The writer of Hebrews then explains that the land promised as an inheritance, this same land promised to Abraham, Isaac and Jacob, is spiritualized or transformed in the New Testament into the inheritance of a heavenly city and heavenly land of the New Covenant (Heb 9:15).

> Hebrews 11:14–16
>
> [14] For people who speak thus make it clear that they are seeking a homeland. [15] If they had been thinking of that land from which they had gone out, they would have had opportunity to return. [16] But as it is, they desire a better country, that is, a heavenly one. Therefore God is not ashamed to be called their God, for he has prepared for them a city [a heavenly city Heb 12:22-24).

In the New Testament, the holy land is a heavenly land, not an earthly one; the holy city Jerusalem is a heavenly city, not an earthly one; the holy temple is a heavenly temple, not an earthly one. Old Covenant earthly shadows find their heavenly realities in New Covenant spirituality (Hebrews 8:5-13). The New Testament transforms the land promise into the new covenant in Christ.

The claim by so-called literalists that "spiritualizing" prophecies is not a legitimate hermeneutic (interpretation) is grossly unbiblical. The New Testament "spiritualizes" all over the place. The sacrifice of Christ on the cross as the "lamb of God" was a spiritualization of the sacrifice of physical lambs in the earthly temple. Jesus was a spiritualized David, not the literal earthly David (Acts 13:34-37). The Body of Christ is the spiritualized temple of God (Eph 2:19-22). And the New Testament claims that the New Covenant Church of united Jew and Gentile believers is also in fact the spiritualized reality of the land promise. Mount Zion, Jerusalem and the temple of the Old Covenant have all been spiritualized into the New Covenant reality of the heavenly Mount Zion, heavenly Jerusalem and heavenly temple.

> Hebrews 12:22–24
>
> [22] But you have come to Mount Zion and to the city of the living God, the heavenly Jerusalem, and to innumerable angels in festal gathering, [23] and to the assembly of the firstborn who are enrolled in heaven, and to God, the judge of all, and to the

spirits of the righteous made perfect, [24] and to Jesus, the mediator of a new covenant.

Ephesians 2:19–22

[19] So then you are no longer strangers and aliens, but you are fellow citizens with the saints and members of the household of God [temple], [20] built on the foundation of the apostles and prophets, Christ Jesus himself being the cornerstone, [21] in whom the whole structure, being joined together, grows into a holy temple in the Lord. [22] In him you also are being built together into a dwelling place for God by the Spirit.

According to the New Testament, the New Covenant Church *is* the heavenly land of promise. The New Covenant Church *is* the heavenly city Jerusalem. The body of Christ on earth *is* the rebuilt heavenly temple. The New Covenant *is* the new heavens and earth, a Scriptural covenantal metaphor (2 Cor 5:17). See my book End Times Bible Prophecy for an explanation of the new heavens and earth.

Ezekiel 37: Resurrection, Regathering, Restoration

But notice one thing at the end of the Ephesians passage above. It says that In Christ, we are "being built up together into a dwelling place for God the Spirit." Not only is this a description of the Church of Jesus Christ as the new holy temple of God on earth, but it is another reference to the prophetic fulfillment of the gathering of Israel and Gentiles as the New Covenant. Follow me on this.

In another place, Paul makes the same spiritual temple analogy of God's dwelling. But notice, he now makes a deliberate quotation from the Old Testament:

2 Corinthians 6:16

[16] For we are the temple of the living God; as God said, "I will make my dwelling among them and walk among them, and I will be their God, and they shall be my people."

Jeremiah 31:31-33 equates this dwelling amidst God's people as the New Covenant. But Ezekiel 37-38 also equates that New Covenant dwelling *with the regathering of Israel*. These elements are all part of the same package. Let's take a look at that prophecy in a bit more detail.

Ezekiel 37:7-14 describes a vision that Ezekiel was given about the regathering and restoration of Israel depicted as a massive resurrection. Then in his further explanation of everything that restoration entailed, he writes this from the mouth of God:

> Ezekiel 37:21–28
>
> [21] then say to them, Thus says the Lord GOD: Behold, <u>I will take the people of Israel from the nations</u> among which they have gone, and will gather them from all around, and bring them to their own land. [22] And <u>I will make them one nation in the land, on the mountains of Israel. And one king shall be king over them all</u>, and they shall be no longer two nations, and no longer divided into two kingdoms… [24] "<u>My servant David shall be king over them, and they shall all have one shepherd.</u> They shall walk in my rules and be careful to obey my statutes. [25] <u>They shall dwell in the land that I gave to my servant Jacob</u>, where your fathers lived. They and their children and their children's children shall dwell there forever, and <u>David my servant shall be their prince forever.</u> [26] <u>I will make a covenant of peace with them. It shall be an everlasting covenant with them.</u> And I will set them in their land and multiply them, and will set my sanctuary in their midst forevermore. [27] <u>My dwelling place shall be with them, and I will be their God, and they shall be my people.</u> [28] Then the nations will know that I am the LORD who sanctifies Israel, when <u>my sanctuary is in their midst forevermore.</u>"

In an expansion of that prophecy earlier in the text, God adds another promise that he will place his spirit within them and give them a heart of flesh to replace their heart of stone (remember the "outpouring of the Spirit" fulfilled in Acts?).

> Ezekiel 36:24–28
>
> [24] I will take you from the nations and gather you from all the countries and bring you into your own land. [25] I will sprinkle clean water on you, and you shall be clean from all your uncleannesses, and from all your idols I will cleanse you. [26] <u>And I will give you a new heart, and a new spirit I will put within you. And I will remove the heart of stone from your flesh and give you a heart of flesh.</u> [27] And I will put my Spirit within you,

and cause you to walk in my statutes and be careful to obey my rules. [28] You shall dwell in the land that I gave to your fathers, and you shall be my people, and I will be your God.

On every level, this entire prophecy is about the arrival of the New Covenant, not some distant future reinstitution of the Old Covenant shadows of physical temple and land. Each of the prophecy's constituent elements are fulfilled in the New Testament Scriptures *at the time of the first century*. Let's take a look at those elements:

1. The gathering of Israel from all the nations (v. 21): This was already explained above as starting to occur in AD 30 at Pentecost (Acts 2). The New Covenant fulfilled in the first century.

2. One nation with one king, David (v. 24-25): It was already detailed above that this messianic reference was Jesus seated on David's throne at his resurrection and ascension (Acts 2:30-33) and uniting his sheepfolds (Jn 10:16). That's the New Covenant fulfilled in the first century.

3. The everlasting covenant of peace with Israel (v. 26): The New Testament says that this everlasting covenant of peace is the New Covenant brought through Christ fulfilled in the first century.

> Hebrews 13:20
> [20] Now may the God of peace who brought again from the dead our Lord Jesus, the great shepherd of the sheep, by the <u>blood of the eternal covenant,</u>
>
> Colossians 1:20
> [20] and through him to reconcile to himself all things, whether on earth or in heaven, making <u>peace by the blood of his cross</u>.

4. God's dwelling place shall be with them (v. 27-28): In multiple places in the New Testament the Church of believers in Jesus are described as God's temple (1Cor 3:16-17; Eph 2:19-22), but Paul explicitly quotes the Ezekiel prophecy of the regathering and God's dwelling as fulfilled in the New Covenant Church beginning in the first century.

> 2 Corinthians 6:16
>
> [16] What agreement has the temple of God with idols? For we are the temple of the living God; <u>as God said, "I will make my dwelling among them and walk among them, and I will be their God, and they shall be my people.</u>

5. Remove the heart of stone, replace with a heart of flesh (36:26): Paul wrote that this promise of heart replacement was fulfilled in the arrival of the New Covenant of Christ fulfilled in the first century.

> 2 Corinthians 3:3
>
> [3] And you show that you are a letter from Christ delivered by us, written not with ink but with the Spirit of the living God, <u>not on tablets of stone but on tablets of human hearts.</u>

6. God will put his Spirit in them and causing them to obey (36:27)

7. He will be their God and they will be His people (36:27): Not only does the Old Testament link these two phrases to the New Covenant (Jer 31:31-34), but the New Testament also claims this promise was fulfilled beginning in the first century with the arrival of the New Covenant.

> Ephesians 1:13
>
> [13] In him you also, when you heard the word of truth, the gospel of your salvation, <u>and believed in him, were sealed with the promised Holy Spirit</u>. (see also Jn 7:37-39, 1Cor 6:19)

> Hebrews 8:6–13
>
> [6] "Behold, the days are coming, declares the Lord, when I will establish a new covenant with the house of Israel and with the house of Judah… <u>I will put my laws into their minds, and write them on their hearts, and I will be their God, and they shall be my people…</u>[13] <u>In speaking of a new covenant, he makes the first one obsolete. And what is becoming obsolete and growing old is ready to vanish away.</u>

Notice how the Holy Spirit-authorized writer of Hebrews says right up front that the promise to the house of Israel and Judah is fulfilled in the arrival of the New Covenant in the first century, *not* in a future time yet to come. God places his Spirit in all believers in Jesus, they are his people of the New Covenant.

Dispensationalists claim that the gathering of the Gentiles occurred with the coming of Jesus but not the promised gathering of Judah and Israel, which has yet to take place. But the New Testament over and over again claims that the New Covenant fulfills that promise to Judah and Israel of their gathering. If the New Testament claims a prophecy has been fulfilled, then it is literally anti-biblical to deny that fulfillment.

Ezekiel 36-37 is pregnant with motifs and promises of the New Covenant arrival of Messiah, not a second coming and reinstitution of Old Covenant shadows. It is important to remember that the Old Testament contains no theology of the second coming of Messiah. It's all about the first coming for them. The second coming is a New Testament doctrine, not an Old Testament one. The whole point to the prophets was that when Messiah came, he would fulfill the promises and usher in the messianic age to come. The New Covenant is that messianic age, complete with Jesus seated on the throne of David (Eph 1:20-23), the regathering of Israel, and the inclusion of the Gentiles, the pouring out of God's Spirit, the new eternal covenant, the replacement of stoney hearts with flesh and God causing his people to walk in his statutes. The whole package is fulfilled in Christ. So when Christians read these prophecies as if they are intended to be split into pieces of fulfillment, the last of which will occur at a second coming of Christ, they are quite simply imposing their preconceived theology onto the text that has already been fulfilled instead of reading it within its original Old Covenant context.

So the natural question arises: How is it that the gathering of Israel could have occurred in the first century, when in fact most of the nation rejected Jesus and even crucified him? That leads us to the theology of the remnant.

The Remnant

So far, I have deliberately avoided a very big qualification in all this talk of the regathering of Israel into the Land. The promise of gathering all the scattered tribes of Israel (and Gentiles) from all the nations sounds like a huge number that would be visibly apparent in history. This causes some to conclude that therefore this event has not happened yet. But that interpretation is based on a false assumption that God meant *all members* of the tribes who were scattered, when he only meant *a remnant* of them. A remnant is a small number out of the whole. That small number was who God was always concerned about. And the helpful thing about it is, he told us this many times in those same prophecies of the ingathering (Amos 9:12; Isa 11:11; Micah 4:1, 7)! Here are just two of them:

> Hosea 1:10–11, 2:23
>
> [10] Yet the number of the children of Israel shall be like the sand of the sea, which cannot be measured or numbered. And in the place where it was said to them, "You are not my people," it shall be said to them, "Children of the living God." [11] And the children of Judah and the children of Israel shall be gathered together, and they shall appoint for themselves one head…[23] and I will sow her for myself in the land. And I will have mercy on No Mercy, and I will say to Not My People, 'You are my people'; and he shall say, 'You are my God.'"

> Isaiah 10:20–22
>
> [20] In that day the remnant of Israel and the survivors of the house of Jacob will no more lean on him who struck them, but will lean on the LORD, the Holy One of Israel, in truth. [21] A remnant will return, the remnant of Jacob, to the mighty God. [22] For though your people Israel be as the sand of the sea, only a remnant of them will return.

Again, notice that the gathering of the remnant and the gathering of the Gentiles ("not my people") are linked together as one event. But the point of it all is that God's promises to Israel as a nation were always made to the remnant of true believers, not to the unbelieving Israelites. What? you may say. It doesn't say "believers vs.

unbelievers." It just says a remnant. That is true. But as we dig deeper, you will see that this remnant is ultimately defined and fulfilled in the New Testament as the true faithful followers of Yahweh. In the same way that Christians often say that just because you belong to a church does not mean you are saved, so in the days of the Old Covenant, belonging to physical earthly Israel did not mean you were the Chosen People of Abraham's children. This is what Paul meant when he wrote, "For not all who are descended from Israel belong to Israel, and not all are children of Abraham because they are his offspring" (Romans 9:6–7). It is only "those who are of faith who are the sons of Abraham" (Gal 3:7), not those who are of the flesh (Gal 4:28-31).

Jesus made this same point that unbelieving Jews were not actually Abraham's children because they did not believe in him as Messiah. In fact, he called them the exact opposite of children of Abraham. He called them children of the devil (Jn 8:39-44). You read that right. *Jesus called physical offspring of Abraham who did not accept him as Messiah children of the devil.*

According to the New Testament, God's promises were always to the faithful, not to the nation as a whole. The rest of the nation merely benefited, went along for the ride, because they were physically with the remnant whom God was blessing.

This theology of the remnant is explained by Paul in Romans 11. He describes the story of Elijah and the prophets of Ba'al on Mount Carmel. Elijah despairs because, with typical prophetic hyperbole, he exclaims that he alone is the only faithful Jew left in an Israel of idolaters. God tells him that he is not. That in fact, God still has seven thousand men who did not bow the knee to Ba'al (Rom 11:1-4).

Paul then concludes,

> Romans 11:5–7 (ESV)
> [5] So too at the present time there is a remnant, chosen by grace.
> [6] But if it is by grace, it is no longer on the basis of works; otherwise grace would no longer be grace. [7] What then? Israel

failed to obtain what it was seeking. The elect obtained it, but the rest were hardened.

So, here we see Paul saying that "at the present time," during his life ministry, there was a remnant of elect chosen out of Israel. And who are those remnant? Obviously Christian believers in Jesus chosen by God's grace through the Gospel (Eph 2:8-10).

But Paul goes farther than merely saying there is a remnant, he actually concludes that that remnant of believers are the remnant of the regathering of Israel prophesied in the very passages of Hosea and Isaiah we quoted above!

> Romans 9:25–27
>
> [23] in order to make known the riches of his glory for vessels of mercy, which he has prepared beforehand for glory— [24] even us whom he has called, <u>not from the Jews only but also from the Gentiles?</u> [25] As indeed he says <u>in Hosea, "Those who were not my people I will call 'my people,'</u> and her who was not beloved I will call 'beloved.' " [26] "And in the very place where it was said to them, 'You are not my people,' there they will be called 'sons of the living God.' " [27] And Isaiah cries out concerning Israel: "<u>Though the number of the sons of Israel be as the sand of the sea, only a remnant of them will be saved</u>

According to Paul, the regathered remnant of the last days prophesied by Isaiah and Hosea and the prophets is the unity of Gentile and Jewish believers in Christ, the mystery of the Gospel occurring at that very moment in history (Eph 3:6). The root of "Israel" in Romans 11 is that remnant of the spiritually faithful, it is not the physical or earthly nation called Israel. Remember, "not all who are descended from Israel belong to Israel" (Rom 9:6-7). Unbelieving earthly Jews are cut off like branches from the root of spiritual Israel, and Gentile believers are grafted onto that spiritual root through faith (Rom 11:13-24). So when he writes that "all Israel will be saved," he is not referring to the physical earthly nation we call Israel, but rather, the spiritual remnant of faithful believers, both Jew and Gentile.

Right after this definition of the remnant, Paul quotes another messianic prophecy that is about the first coming of Messiah.

> Romans 11:26–27
> [26] And in this way all Israel will be saved, as it is written, "The Deliverer will come from Zion, he will banish ungodliness from Jacob"; [27] "and this will be my covenant with them when I take away their sins."

Those who think this "Israel" is an earthly geopolitical nation rather than the spiritually faithful remnant have to make that verse apply to a future second coming of Christ. But their problem is that it is the first coming of Messiah bringing the New Covenant that saves both Jew and Gentile alike through faith. And remember, the theology of the remnant proves that God was not speaking of the physical earthly descendants of Abraham, he was talking of the true spiritual Israel; believers in Messiah. The covenant that takes away Israel's sins is the New Covenant (Jer 31:31-34). All Israel being saved is not a future prophecy of an earthly nation, it is the declaration of the Gospel: "In this way [of faith in Messiah], all Israel [both Jew and Gentile believer] will be saved."

So, if it is only a remnant who are saved, what happens to the rest of unbelieving Israel? Jesus and the apostles are clear in their proclamation that the rest of the Jewish nation will be judged and cast out from the New Covenant kingdom. That judgment consisted of the destruction of their holy city and temple (See my End Times Bible Prophecy for a full explanation of this destruction).

Isaiah foretold this destruction of unbelieving Jews in correlation with the ingathering of the remnant at the feast of Messiah's kingdom (the New Covenant).

> Isaiah 65:8–16
> [8] Thus says the LORD: ...So I will do for my servants' sake, and not destroy them all... [11]But you who forsake the LORD... [12]I will destine you to the sword, and all of you shall bow down

to the slaughter, because, when I called, you did not answer; when I spoke, you did not listen,..."Behold, my servants shall eat, but you shall be hungry; behold, my servants shall drink, but you shall be thirsty; behold, my servants shall rejoice, but you shall be put to shame;... [15] You shall leave your name to my chosen for a curse, and the Lord GOD will put you to death, but his servants he will call by another name [Christian].

Jesus told three parables that echoed this Isaianic motif of destruction/remnant/feast in the coming desolation of Jerusalem and the temple in AD 70. God delivers his remnant and destroys the rest. The parable of the tenants describes the first century Jews (tenants of the vineyard) killing God's son. Jesus concludes that God (the owner of the vineyard) will come and "he will put those wretches to a miserable death and let out the vineyard to other tenants who will give him the fruits in their seasons" (Matt 21:41).

In the parable of the wedding feast, Jesus compared the kingdom of God to a wedding feast of a king, and the Gospel to the invitation for that feast. But the first century Jewish unbelievers did not accept the wedding invitation (the Gospel), and instead killed God's servants who called them (prophets and apostles). He concludes, "The king was angry, and he sent his troops and destroyed those murderers and burned their city [Jerusalem]." Then the king (God) said to his servants (Jewish believers), 'The wedding feast is ready, but those invited were not worthy'" (Matt 22:7-8). He then offers the invite to anyone they could find (the Gentiles).

The third parable of the master of the house has Jesus likening unbelieving Jews to those who think that they know God but who actually do not, and would be rejected at the coming kingdom feast (the New Covenant consummation). That kingdom feast is considered as part of the gathering of the remnant from the four corners of the earth (Isa 43:5-7).

Luke 13:27–29

[27] But he will say, 'I tell you, I do not know where you come from. Depart from me, all you workers of evil!' [28] In that place

there will be weeping and gnashing of teeth, when you see Abraham and Isaac and Jacob and all the prophets in the kingdom of God <u>but you yourselves cast out. [29] And people will come from east and west, and from north and south, and recline at table in the kingdom of God.</u> (see also Matt 8:11-12)

These parables all reinforce Jesus' prediction of the AD 70 temple destruction in his Olivet Discourse:

> Matthew 23:37–24:2 (ESV)
> [37] "O Jerusalem, Jerusalem, the city that kills the prophets and stones those who are sent to it! <u>How often would I have gathered your children together</u> as a hen gathers her brood under her wings, <u>and you were not willing!</u> [38] <u>See, your house is left to you desolate…</u>[1] Jesus left the temple and was going away, when his disciples came to point out to him the buildings of the temple. [2] But he answered them, "You see all these, do you not? <u>Truly, I say to you, there will not be left here one stone upon another that will not be thrown down</u>."

The apostle Paul reinforced this casting off of unbelieving Israel when he told his own allegory of Abraham's children from two different wives, Sarah and Hagar in Galatians 4:21-31. As already explained above in chapter 3 on the children of Abraham, Paul likened unbelieving Jews of the first century to mere Old Covenant children of the flesh, but not inheritors of the Promise to Abraham in the New Covenant (v. 24-26). The children of promise (the remnant) he describes as the Jewish believers in Jesus, who were presently being persecuted by the unbelieving Jews of his day (v. 30-31). The Jewish Christians were the children of the free woman, and the unbelieving Jews were children of the slave woman. And those unbelieving Jews would be cast out from the inheritance of the kingdom of God (inheritance as a metaphor for the Land promise), while the remnant alone would inherit the kingdom.

> Galatians 4:30–31
> [30] But what does the Scripture say? "Cast out the slave woman and her son, for the son of the slave woman shall not inherit with the son of the free woman." [31] So, brothers, we are not children of the slave but of the free woman.

So God's delivery of the remnant was always tied to the gathering of Israel, as well as the ingathering of the Gentiles, as well as the judgment of the rest of unbelieving Jews and their casting out. God would bring in his New Covenant kingdom, judge those Jews who rejected Messiah by destroying their city and temple, but rescue his remnant believers (Christians). This is exactly what happened in AD 70 when Roman armies destroyed Jerusalem and the Christians escaped to the mountains.

For a detailed comparison of all the Old Testament prophecies of the gathering of the remnant of Israel fulfilled in the New Testament, see my Matthew 24 Fulfilled: Biblical and Historical Sources. It is a compendium of my notes on Matthew 24 and the Last Days.

The 144,000

Interpreting the book of Revelation is a complex task. To focus on any one element is sure to raise a dozen questions about other aspects of the apocalypse and its interwoven tapestry of events and theology. But I wanted to finish this chapter on the gathering of the remnant by addressing its presence in the eschatological conclusion of the New Testament.

I subscribe to a preterist interpretation of Revelation. That means that I believe its main purpose is not to speak of the end of time or end of the world, but rather to declare the final judgment upon the Jews for rejecting and murdering their Messiah (Rev 1:7), and to affirm the divorce of Old Covenant Israel with God's marriage to the New Covenant bride of Christ (Rev 21). This is achieved through the prediction of the desolation of Jerusalem and the temple by the Roman armies of Titus in AD 70. By destroying the earthly elements of the Old Covenant, God was dissolving that Old Covenant and replacing it with the New Covenant in real historical time. Therefore, the apostle John was warning the Jewish Christians, who he considered God's chosen remnant, the symbolic 144,000, to get out of Jerusalem and out of the surrounding cities before the wrath of God arrived on the unbelievers. This view is explained in more detail in my book, End Times Bible Prophecy: It's Not What They Told You.

Within this context, the 144,000 from the twelve tribes, is the consummating fulfillment of the regathering of remnant believing Israel.

> Revelation 7:2–4
>
> [2] Then I saw another angel ascending from the rising of the sun, with the seal of the living God, and he called with a loud voice to the four angels who had been given power to harm earth and sea, [3] saying, "Do not harm the earth or the sea or the trees, until we have sealed the servants of our God on their foreheads." [4] And I heard the number of the sealed, 144,000, sealed from every tribe of the sons of Israel:
>
> Revelation 14:1, 4
>
> [1] Then I looked, and behold, on Mount Zion stood the Lamb, and with him 144,000 who had his name and his Father's name written on their foreheads…[4] It is these who follow the Lamb wherever he goes. These have been redeemed from mankind as firstfruits for God and the Lamb.

It is beyond the scope of this booklet to exegete all the details of this passage. But let me just point out that the sealing of the 144,000 represents God's ownership and protection over them in contrast with the condemned who are sealed with the Mark of the Beast (Rev 13:16-18). The reference to the twelve tribes indicates not only that this is the regathering of the remnant out of Mount Zion/Jerusalem (Isa 37:31-32), but that they are the Jewish Christians in Israel who were protected from the wrath that was coming upon the land and city in AD 70. They were the ones who fled to the mountains to escape the abomination of desolation, just as Jesus had told them to (Matt 24:15-21). The 144,000 are also described as "first-fruits for God and the Lamb" (14:4), a phrase that indicates they were the first Christian converts of that generation who were in Jerusalem (Acts 2).

This remnant of course is not exhaustive, for the text right after this gathering then adds the inclusion of the Gentiles, that other element so often found together with the regathering in Old Testament prophecies.

> Revelation 7:9–14
>
> [9] After this I looked, and behold, a great multitude that no one could number, from every nation, from all tribes and peoples and languages, standing before the throne and before the Lamb, clothed in white robes, with palm branches in their hands, [10] and crying out with a loud voice, "Salvation belongs to our God who sits on the throne, and to the Lamb!"…And he said to me, "These are the ones coming out of the great tribulation. They have washed their robes and made them white in the blood of the Lamb.

Followers of Jesus the Lamb "from every nation and tribe" means "from the Gentiles." There it is again. The regathering of Israel's true remnant believers *alongside* the ingathering of the Gentiles to make one unity in the body of Christ (Eph 3:4-6). The regathering of Israel and the ingathering of the Gentiles are almost always spoken of as being together. In other words, they are two sides of one activity of God. He does not separate them in time as the Dispensationalist claims. They are two actions of one Gospel.

But the 144,000 came out of the "great tribulation." Many Christians read this with their preconceived bias that the tribulation is an event in our future. But their problem is that the Scripture says the tribulation *is actually in our past*. The apostle John had written that the great tribulation was already going on in the first century, and he was a partaker in it with Gentile Christians all over the empire (especially the churches of Asia Minor – Rev 2-3).

> Revelation 1:9
>
> I, John, your brother and <u>partner in the tribulation</u> and the kingdom…

You can't get any more biblical than that. The Apostle John saying that he was going through the Tribulation as he wrote the book of Revelation! The Tribulation is not in our future. It was in John's day.

It so happens, that during that time that John was writing, approximately AD 65, the Neronic persecution of Christians was in full tilt, which was followed by the Roman invasion and destruction of the land of Israel, its holy city Jerusalem and temple in AD 70.

Wait a second. Didn't Jesus say the Tribulation was "such as has not been from the beginning of the world until now, no, and never will be"? How could John have been referring to the first century if that was not the greatest of all historical tribulations?

The answer is quite simple. The phrase is common ancient Hebrew hyperbole that was used to describe the spiritual ramifications of an historical event. Daniel used the same exact phrase when he described the first destruction of Jerusalem and the temple in 586 BC.

> Daniel 9:12 (ESV)
> For under the whole heaven there has not been done anything like what has been done against Jerusalem.

Ezekiel also used the same hyperbole when describing the same destruction of city and temple:

> Ezekiel 5:9 (ESV)
> And because of all [Israel's] abominations I will do with you what I have never yet done, and the like of which I will never do again.

Does God contradict himself? Was the first destruction of the city and temple any greater than the destruction of the city and temple in AD 70? Of course not. It was a way of describing the same kind of spiritual devastation that occurred in both time periods. This is akin to our saying, "I've never seen anything like it!" when in fact, we have. There is nothing more serious in its spiritual ramifications than the destruction of the incarnation of God's covenant with Israel.

Flee to the Mountains

But that's not all. Because Jesus said something right before he warned about the great tribulation that was coming within the lifetime of his hearers (Matt 23:36; 24:34). He told the Jewish Christians who lived in Judea to flee to the mountains.

> Matthew 24:16–20 (ESV)
> [16] then let those who are in Judea flee to the mountains. [17] Let the one who is on the housetop not go down to take what is in his house, [18] and let the one who is in the field not turn back to take his cloak. [19] And alas for women who are pregnant and for those who are nursing infants in those days! [20] Pray that your flight may not be in winter or on a Sabbath.

Fleeing to the mountains would be of no effect in our modern world, where there is no geographical "safe space" in Israel. But in the first century, when the Romans were surrounding Jerusalem with their armies, there was. It would make sense for Christians to get out of the city and flee to the mountains to avoid the wrath about to come.

And that's exactly what they did. Reputable ancient Church historian, Eusebius tells us:

> But the people of the church in Jerusalem had been commanded by a revelation, vouchsafed to approved men there before the war, to leave the city and to dwell in a certain town of Perea called Pella. And when those that believed in Christ had come thither from Jerusalem, then, as if the royal city of the Jews and the whole land of Judea were entirely destitute of holy men, the judgment of God at length overtook those who had committed such outrages against Christ and his apostles, and totally destroyed that generation of impious men.[2]

This all fits with a "preterist" interpretation of the book of Revelation as being fulfilled in our past. Revelation's main purpose is not to speak of the end of time or end of the world, but rather to declare the final judgment upon the Jews for rejecting and murdering their Messiah (Rev 1:7), and to affirm the divorce of Old Covenant Israel with God's marriage to the New Covenant bride of Christ (Rev 21). This was achieved through the desolation of Jerusalem and the temple

---

[2] Eusebius of Caesaria, "The Church History of Eusebius," in *Eusebius: Church History, Life of Constantine the Great, and Oration in Praise of Constantine*, ed. Philip Schaff and Henry Wace, trans. Arthur Cushman McGiffert, vol. 1, A Select Library of the Nicene and Post-Nicene Fathers of the Christian Church, Second Series (New York: Christian Literature Company, 1890), 138.

by the Roman armies of Titus in AD 70. By destroying the earthly elements of the Old Covenant, God was dissolving that Old Covenant and replacing it with the New Covenant in real historical time.

Symbolic Number

So the 144,000 were the Jewish Christians in first-century Israel, and more particularly in the city of Jerusalem, who were protected from God's wrath by leaving the city and fleeing to the mountains before it was destroyed by the Romans in AD 70.

Was there exactly 144,000 or was that merely symbolic? It doesn't really matter. There were so few Christians at that time period that it might have been for all we know. Though the biblical usage of numbers like 12 tribes multiplied by 12 apostles multiplied by 1000, the number of perfect completion, is a little too obvious to deny.

The tribulation was already ongoing when John wrote the Revelation. The gathering of the persecuted remnant with the Gentiles all over the empire was the beginning creation of the body of Christ that would soon spread the Gospel beyond Jerusalem and Samaria to the ends of the earth (Acts 1:8). Particularly in the holy land, the Christians were spared and earthly Israel was judged. Of course there is more to it than that, but at least the reader can get an idea of the big picture narrative and how it all fits into the fulfillment of the promised remnant regathering. For all the details of how Revelation was fulfilled in the first century, see Kenneth Gentry's game-changing commentary, *The Divorce of Israel: A Redemptive-Historical Interpretation of Revelation* (GA: Tolle Lege Press, 2017).

This brief excursion into the theology of the regathering of the remnant of Israel illustrates just how poetic, beautiful and glorious the New Covenant is, just how true and real the heavenly land, city and temple is as embodied in the Body of Christ, his Church. The Bible is not a racist document that maintains the eternal superiority of a single geopolitical nation or chance genetic birth of a single ethnic demographic. In all corners of the Old Testament, God foretold that he would one day transform his Old Covenant with a New Covenant that would draw peoples from every tribe and nation into covenant with the Messiah of all the earth. Amen.

11
Old Testament Shadow, New Testament Reality

This table below is a verse-by-verse comparison of how the New Testament illustrates that the Church of Jesus Christ is the true Israel of God. Every term used in the Old Testament that Dispensationalists think applies to physical Israel according to the flesh, is actually applied to the Christian Church according to the Spirit. There cannot be two plans or two God's people when one of them fulfills it all. This is not a "replacement" of Israel with the Church, for the Church ("congregation of the Lord") that consists of both Jew and Gentile believers, *is* Israel regathered as a remnant in the New Covenant. The Old Covenant land, city and temple were mere shadows of the heavenly reality in New Covenant Christ.

Old Testament Shadow	Biblical Term	New Testament Reality
Genesis 17:5 "No longer shall your name be called Abram, But your name shall be Abraham; For I will make you the father of a multitude of nations. 6 "And I will make you exceedingly fruitful, and I will make nations of you, and kings shall come forth from you. 7 "And I will establish My covenant between Me and you and your descendants after you throughout their generations for an	Children of Abraham	Galatians 3:6–9 [6] just as Abraham "believed God, and it was counted to him as righteousness"? [7] Know then that it is **those of faith who are the sons of Abraham**. [8] And the Scripture, foreseeing that God would justify the Gentiles by faith, preached the gospel beforehand to Abraham, saying, "In you shall all the nations be blessed." [9] So then, those who are of faith are blessed along with Abraham, the man of faith.

everlasting covenant, to be God to you and to your descendants after you. (Also Gen 11:1-3)		(Also Rom 4:13-17; Gal 3:29)
Genesis 17:19 But God said, "No, but Sarah your wife shall bear you a son, and you shall call his name Isaac; and **I will establish My covenant with him for an everlasting covenant for his descendants after him.** (Also Gen 17:5-7) Genesis 21: 10 Therefore she said to Abraham, "Drive out this maid and her son, for the son of this maid shall not be an heir with my son Isaac." 11 And the matter distressed Abraham greatly because of his son. 12 But God said to Abraham, "Do not be distressed because of the lad and your maid; whatever Sarah tells you, listen to her, for through Isaac your descendants shall be named. 13 "And of the son of the maid I will make a nation also, because he is your descendant." Isaiah 54: 1 "Shout for joy, O barren one, you who have borne no child; Break forth into joyful shouting and cry aloud, you who have not travailed; For the sons of the desolate one will be more numerous Than the sons of the married woman," says the LORD. ...3 "For you will spread abroad to the right and to the left. And your descendants will possess nations, And they will resettle the desolate cities.	**Children of Promise**	Romans 9:8 [8] This means that it is not the children of the flesh who are the children of God, but the **children of the promise** are counted as offspring. (Also Joh 1:12; Joh 11:52; Ro 8:16) Galatians 4:24–31 [24] Now this may be interpreted allegorically: these women are two covenants. One is from Mount Sinai, bearing children for slavery; she is Hagar. [25] Now Hagar is Mount Sinai in Arabia; she corresponds to the present Jerusalem, for she is in slavery with her children. [26] But the Jerusalem above is free, and she is our mother. [27] For it is written, "Rejoice, O barren one who does not bear; break forth and cry aloud, you who are not in labor! For the children of the desolate one will be more than those of the one who has a husband." [28] **Now you, brothers, like Isaac, are children of promise**. [29] But just as at that time he who was born according to the flesh persecuted him who was born according to the Spirit, so also it is now. [30] But what does the Scripture say? "Cast out the slave woman and her son, for the son of the slave woman shall not inherit with the son of the free woman." [31] So, brothers, **we are not children of the slave but of the free woman.**
Exodus 19:6 and you shall be to Me a kingdom of priests and a **holy nation.**' These are the words that you shall speak to the sons of Israel."	**Holy Nation**	1 Peter 2:9 [9] But you are a chosen race, a royal priesthood, **a holy nation**, a people for his own possession,

Exodus 19:6 and you shall be to Me a **kingdom of priests** and a holy nation.' These are the words that you shall speak to the sons of Israel."	Royal Priesthood	1 Peter 2:9 ⁹ But you are a chosen race, **a royal priesthood**, a holy nation, a people for his own possession,
Deuteronomy 7:6 "For you are a holy people to the LORD your God; the LORD your God has chosen you to be **a people for His own possession** out of all the peoples who are on the face of the earth. (Also De 4:20)	People for God's Own Possession	1 Peter 2:9 ⁹ But you are a chosen race, a royal priesthood, a holy nation, **a people for his own possession**,
Isaiah 43:20 "The beasts of the field will glorify Me; ... Because I have given waters in the wilderness And rivers in the desert, To give drink to **My chosen people**.(Also De 7:6; 14:2; Isa 45:4)	Chosen People	1 Peter 2:9 ⁹ But you are **a chosen race**, a royal priesthood, a holy nation, a people for his own possession, (Also Col 3:12; Re 17:14)
Isaiah 24:23 For the LORD of hosts will reign on **Mount Zion** and in Jerusalem, And His glory will be before His elders. Zechariah 8:3 "Thus says the LORD, 'I will return to **Zion** and will dwell in the midst of Jerusalem. Then Jerusalem will be called the City of Truth, and the mountain of the LORD of hosts will be called the **Holy Mountain**.'	Mount Zion	Hebrews 12:22–24 ²² But you have come to **Mount Zion** and to the city of the living God, the heavenly Jerusalem, and to innumerable angels in festal gathering, ²³ and to the assembly of the firstborn who are enrolled in heaven, and to God, the judge of all, and to the spirits of the righteous made perfect, ²⁴ and to Jesus, the mediator of a new covenant, and to the sprinkled blood that speaks a better word than the blood of Abel.
Zechariah 8:3 "Thus says the LORD, 'I will return to Zion and will dwell in the midst of Jerusalem. Then **Jerusalem** will be called the City of Truth, and the mountain of the LORD of hosts will be called the Holy Mountain.' (Also Zec 1:17; Mic 4:2)	Jerusalem	Hebrews 12:22–24 ²² But you have come to Mount Zion and to the city of the living God, **the heavenly Jerusalem**, and to innumerable angels in festal gathering, ²³ and to the assembly of the firstborn who are enrolled in heaven.
Isaiah 44:21 "Remember these things, O Jacob, And Israel, for you are My servant; I have formed you, you are My servant, O Israel, you will	Israel	Galatians 6:15 For neither is circumcision anything, nor uncircumcision, but a new creation. 16 And those who will walk by this rule, peace and

not be forgotten by Me. Isaiah 45:17 Israel has been saved by the LORD With an everlasting salvation; You will not be put to shame or humiliated To all eternity. Jeremiah 10:16 The portion of Jacob is not like these; For the Maker of all is He, And Israel is the tribe of His inheritance; The LORD of hosts is His name.		mercy be upon them, and upon the **Israel of God**. Romans 9:6 But it is not as though the word of God has failed. For they are **not all Israel who are descended from Israel**; Ephesians 2:12 Remember that you were at that time separate from Christ, excluded from the **commonwealth of Israel**, and strangers to the covenants of promise, ... But now in Christ Jesus you who formerly were far off have been brought near by the blood of Christ. 14 For He Himself is our peace, who **made both groups into one, and broke down the barrier of the dividing wall**, 15 by abolishing in His flesh the enmity, which is the Law of commandments contained in ordinances, that in Himself He **might make the two into one new man**,
Jeremiah 31:31 "Behold, days are coming," declares the LORD, "when I will make a **new covenant with the house of Israel** and with the house of Judah, 32 not like the covenant which I made with their fathers in the day I took them by the hand to bring them out of the land of Egypt, My covenant which they broke, although I was a husband to them, "declares the LORD. 33 "But this is the covenant which I will make with the house of Israel after those days," declares the LORD, "I will put My law within them, and on their heart I will write it; and I will be their God, and they shall be My people. 34 "And they shall not teach again, each man his neighbor and each man his brother, saying, 'Know the LORD,' for they shall all know Me, from the least of them to the greatest of them," declares the LORD, "for I will forgive their	New Covenant	Hebrews 8:6–13 ⁶ But as it is, Christ has obtained a ministry that is as **much more excellent than the old as the covenant he mediates is better**, since it is enacted on better promises. ⁷ For if that first covenant had been faultless, there would have been no occasion to look for a second. ⁸ For he finds fault with them when he says: "Behold, the days are coming, declares the Lord, **when I will establish a new covenant** with the house of Israel and with the house of Judah, ⋯ **For this is the covenant that I will make with the house of Israel** after those days, declares the Lord: I will put my laws into their minds, and write them on their hearts, and I will be their God, and they shall be my people. ¹¹ And they shall not teach, each one his neighbor and each one his brother, saying, 'Know the Lord,' for they shall all know me, from the least of them to the

iniquity, and their sin I will remember no more."		greatest. [12] For I will be merciful toward their iniquities, and I will remember their sins no more." [13] **In speaking of a new covenant, he makes the first one obsolete**. And what is becoming obsolete and growing old is ready to vanish away.
Psalm 46:4 There is a river whose streams make glad the **city of God,** The holy dwelling places of the Most High. Ps 87:3 Glorious things are spoken of you, O **city of God.**	City of God	Hebrews 12:22 But you have come to Mount Zion and to the **city of the living God,** the heavenly Jerusalem, and to myriads of angels...
Deuteronomy 30: 6 "Moreover the LORD your God will **circumcise your heart** and the heart of your descendants, to love the LORD your God. Jeremiah 4:4 "**Circumcise** yourselves to the LORD And **remove the foreskins of your heart**, Men of Judah and inhabitants of Jerusalem... Jeremiah 9:25 "Behold, the days are coming," declares the LORD, "that I will punish **all who are circumcised and yet uncircumcised**...for all the nations are uncircumcised, and all the house of Israel are **uncircumcised of heart**."	Circumcised Heart	Romans 2: 28 For he is not a Jew who is one outwardly; neither is circumcision that which is outward in the flesh. 29 **But he is a Jew who is one inwardly; and circumcision is that which is of the heart,** by the Spirit, not by the letter; and his praise is not from men, but from God. Colossians 2:11 and **in Him you were also circumcised with a circumcision made without hands,** in the removal of the body of the flesh by the circumcision of Christ;
Isaiah 10:22-23 For though your people, O Israel, may be like the sand of the sea, Only a **remnant within them will return**; A destruction is determined, overflowing with righteousness. For a complete destruction, one that is decreed, the Lord GOD of hosts will execute in the midst of the whole land. Isaiah 46:3 "Listen to Me, O house of Jacob, And **all the remnant of the house of Israel**, You who have	Remnant	Romans 9:27–29 [27] And Isaiah cries out concerning Israel: "Though the number of the sons of Israel be as the sand of the sea, **only a remnant of them will be saved**, [28] for the Lord will carry out his sentence upon the earth fully and without delay." [29] And as Isaiah predicted, "**If the Lord of hosts had not left us offspring**, we would have been like Sodom and become like Gomorrah." Romans 11:1-7 I say then, God has not rejected

been borne by Me from birth, And have been carried from the womb; Jeremiah 23:3-6 "Then I Myself shall gather the **remnant of My flock** out of all the countries where I have driven them and shall bring them back to their pasture; and they will be fruitful and multiply..."Behold, the days are coming," declares the LORD, "When **I shall raise up for David a righteous Branch;** [Jesus] And He will reign as king and act wisely And do justice and righteousness in the land. "**In His days Judah will be saved, And Israel will dwell securely**;		His people, has He? May it never be!...God has not rejected His people whom He foreknew....In the same way then, there has also come to be at the present time a **remnant according to God's gracious choice**... What then? That which Israel is seeking for, it has not obtained, but **those who were chosen obtained it**, and the rest were hardened; 1Peter 1:1 Peter, an apostle of Jesus Christ, to those who reside as aliens, scattered..who are **chosen**]
2Chronicles 7:14 and My people who are called by My name humble themselves and pray, Hosea 1:10 Yet the number of the sons of **Israel** Will be like the sand of the sea, Which cannot be measured or numbered; And it will come about that, in the place Where it is said to them, "**You are not My people**," It will be said to them, "**You are the sons of the living God**." Jeremiah 31:33 "But this is the covenant which I will make with the house of Israel after those days," declares the LORD, "I will put My law within them, and on their heart I will write it; and I will be their God, **and they shall be My people**.	My People Called by My Name	Acts 15:17 [17] that the remnant of mankind may seek the Lord, and all the **Gentiles who are called by my name**, says the Lord Romans 9:25–26 [25] As indeed he says in Hosea, "Those who were not my people I will call 'my people,' and her who was not beloved I will call 'beloved.' " [26] "And in the very place where it was said to them, 'You are not my people,' there they will be called 'sons of the living God.' " 2 Corinthians 6:16 [16] God said, "I will make my dwelling among them and walk among them, **and I will be their God, and they shall be my people**.
Exodus 29:45 "And **I will dwell among** the sons of Israel and will be their God. 46 "And they shall know that I am the LORD their God who brought them out of the land of Egypt, that **I might dwell among them**; I am the LORD their God. Leviticus 26:12	Temple, God's Dwelling Place	Ephesians 2:19–22 [19] So then you are no longer strangers and aliens, but you are fellow citizens with the saints and members of the **household of God**, [20] **built on the foundation** of the apostles and prophets, Christ Jesus himself being the cornerstone, [21] **in whom the whole structure, being joined together,**

Israel	Biblical Term	Fulfilled in Christ
'I will also walk among you and be your God, and you shall be My people. Exodus 25:8 "And let them construct a sanctuary for Me, **that I may dwell among them**.		**grows into a holy temple in the Lord. [22] In him you also are being built together into a dwelling place for God by the Spirit.** 2 Corinthians 6:16 [16] For **we are the temple of the living God**; as God said, "**I will make my dwelling among them** and walk among them, and I will be their God, and they shall be my people.
Israel	**Biblical Term**	**Fulfilled in Christ**
Genesis 17:8 "And I will give to you [Abraham] and to your offspring after you **the land** of your sojournings, **all the** land of Canaan, for an everlasting possession."	The Land Promise to Abraham	2 Corinthians 1:20 For **all the promises of God find their Yes in him [Jesus].** Hebrews 11:8–10 By faith Abraham obeyed when he was called to go out to a place that he was to receive as an inheritance. And he went out, not knowing where he was going. **By faith he went to live in the land of promise,** as in a foreign land, living in tents with Isaac and Jacob, heirs with him of the same promise. **For he was looking forward to the city that has foundations, whose designer and builder is God.** Hebrews 11:15–16 If they had been thinking of that land from which they had gone out, they would have had opportunity to return. But as it is, **they desire a better country, that is, a heavenly one.** Therefore God is not ashamed to be called their God, **for he has prepared for them a city**. Hebrews 12:22–24 **But you have come to Mount Zion and to the city of the living God, the heavenly Jerusalem... and to Jesus, the mediator of a new covenant.** [Jesus is Mount Zion, heavenly Jerusalem]

Deuteronomy 30:3 then the Lord your God will restore your fortunes and have mercy on you, and **he will gather you again from all the peoples where the Lord your God has scattered you.**	Restoration to the Land	Acts 2:5–11 [Pentecost was the fulfillment of gathering the Jews "from all the nations" into the land—but in Christ that is fulfilled] Now there were dwelling in Jerusalem **Jews, devout men from every nation under heaven**…"Are not all these who are speaking Galileans? And how is it that we hear, each of us in his own native language? Parthians and Medes and Elamites and residents of Mesopotamia, Judea and Cappadocia, Pontus and Asia, Phrygia and Pamphylia, Egypt and the parts of Libya belonging to Cyrene, and visitors from Rome, both Jews and proselytes, Cretans and Arabians—we hear them telling in our own tongues the mighty works of God."
Ezekiel 37:12 "Thus says the Lord God: Behold, I will open your graves and raise you from your graves, O my people. And **I will bring you into the land of Israel.**" Deuteronomy 32:8–9 When the Most High **gave to the nations their inheritance**, when he divided mankind, **he fixed the borders of the peoples** according to the number of the sons of God. But the Lord's portion is his people, Jacob his allotted heritage.	Resurrection of Israel = receiving the Land inheritance	1 Peter 1:3–4 According to his great mercy, he has caused us to be born again to a living hope **through the resurrection of Jesus Christ from the dead, to an inheritance that is imperishable, undefiled, and unfading, kept in heaven for you**. Hebrews 9:15 Therefore he is the mediator of a new covenant, so that those who are called may receive the **promised eternal inheritance**
Genesis 17:8 "And I will give to you [Abraham] and to your **offspring [seed]** after you the land of your sojournings, all the land of Canaan, for an everlasting possession."	The Seed Promise to Abraham	Galatians 3:16 Now the promises were made to Abraham and to his offspring [seed]. It does not say, "And to offsprings," referring to many, but referring to one, "**And to your offspring**," who is Christ.
Ezekiel 43:7 "Son of man, **this is the place of my throne…where I will dwell in the midst of the people of Israel** forever.	The Temple	John 1:14 **And the Word became flesh and dwelt** [tabernacled=temple] among us, and we have seen his glory.

		John 2:19–21 Jesus answered them, "Destroy this temple, and in three days I will raise it up." The Jews then said, "It has taken forty-six years to build this temple, and will you raise it up in three days?" **But he was speaking about the temple of his body.** Revelation 21:22
Isaiah 41:8–9 But you, Israel, my servant, Jacob, whom I have chosen, the offspring of Abraham, my friend; you whom I took from the ends of the earth, and called from its farthest corners, saying to you, "You are my servant, I have chosen you and not cast you off" Isaiah 53:1 Who has believed what he has heard from us? And to whom has the arm of the Lord been revealed? Isaiah 53:7–8 He was oppressed, and he was afflicted, yet he opened not his mouth; like a lamb that is led to the slaughter, and like a sheep that before its shearers is silent, so he opened not his mouth…he was cut off out of the land of the living, stricken for the transgression of my people Isaiah 53:12 Therefore I will divide him [My Servant] a portion with the many, and he shall divide the spoil with the strong, because he poured out his soul to death and was numbered with the transgressors; yet he bore the sin of many, and makes intercession for the transgressors.	**My Servant = Israel** **Jesus is therefore Israel**	Matthew 8:16–17 That evening they brought to him many who were oppressed by demons, and he cast out the spirits with a word and healed all who were sick. **This was to fulfill what was spoken by the prophet Isaiah: "He took our illnesses and bore our diseases."** John 12:38 so that the word spoken by the prophet Isaiah might be fulfilled: "Lord, who has believed what he heard from us, and to whom has the arm of the Lord been revealed?" Acts 8:32–33 (ESV) Now the passage of the Scripture that he was reading was this: "Like a sheep he was led to the slaughter and like a lamb before its shearer is silent, so he opens not his mouth. In his humiliation justice was denied him. Luke 22:37 "For I tell you that this Scripture must be fulfilled in me: 'And he was numbered with the transgressors.' For what is written about me has its fulfillment."

Get the Theology behind Chronicles of the Apocalypse

The Biblical Theology behind Chronicles of the Apocalypse
By Brian Godawa

    Brian Godawa reveals the Biblical and historical basis for the Last Days presented in the novel series *Chronicles of the Apocalypse*.
    Godawa unveils the biblical meaning of many End Times notions like the Last Days, cosmic catastrophes, the Abomination of Desolation, the antichrist, the Great Tribulation, and more!
Available in eBook, Paperback & Audiobook

Click Here For Details
https://wp.me/P6y1ub-io8

Are We Living in the Last Days?
Check out this Controversial Online Course!

25% OFF!
Limited Time Only
10+ Intense Lectures on End Times
Powerpoint Videos with Powerful Visuals By Brian Godawa

There are so many Christians teaching outrageous things about Bible Prophecy these days. It's enough to frustrate the serious Bible student. What would you think if you found out most all of it is simply mistaken? What if you found out that the ancient mindset of the Jewish writers was influenced by the Old Testament imagery of the past, and not a crystal ball gaze into our modern future? What if you found out that everything that modern prophecy pundits are looking for—the antichrist, the Beast, the Tribulation, the Rapture—was not what they told you it was, but something different?

Includes lots of colorful and helpful PowerPoint visuals, charts, pictures, and film clips for a much richer presentation of the material.

PLUS a bunch of FREE Bonuses!

Check out the Free Introduction & Learn More
(Use Code NTBA84 for 25% Discount)

Click Here For Details

LastDaysCourse.com

Get More Biblical Imagination

Get More Biblical Imagination

Sign up Online For The Godawa Chronicles

www.Godawa.com

Insider information on the novels of Brian Godawa

Special Discounts, New Releases,

Bible Mysteries!

We won't spam you.

Chronicles of the Nephilim

Nephilim Giants, Watchers, Cosmic War. Novels From the Bible.
www.Godawa.com

Chronicles of the Apocalypse

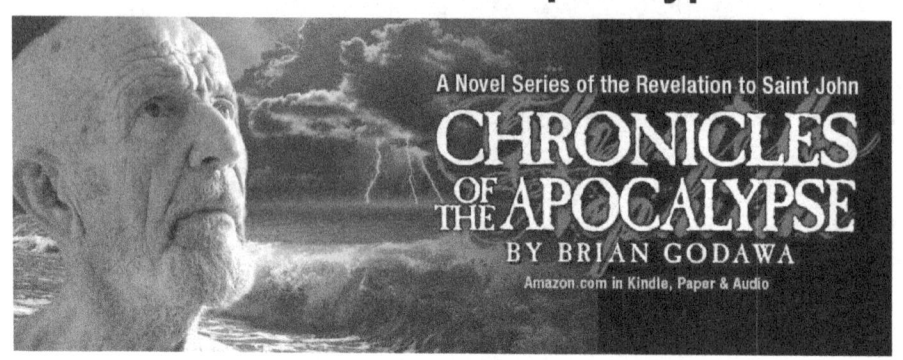

A Novel Series About
the Book of Revelation & the End Times.
A Fresh Biblical View.

www.Godawa.com

Chronicles of the Watchers

A Series About the Watchers in History. Action, Romance, Gods, Monsters & Men.

The first novel is *Jezebel: Harlot Queen of Israel.*

www.Godawa.com

About The Author

Brian Godawa is the screenwriter for the award-winning feature film, *To End All Wars,* starring Kiefer Sutherland. It was awarded the Commander in Chief Medal of Service, Honor and Pride by the Veterans of Foreign Wars, won the first Heartland Film Festival by storm, and showcased the Cannes Film Festival Cinema for Peace.

He also co-wrote *Alleged*, starring Brian Dennehy as Clarence Darrow and Fred Thompson as William Jennings Bryan. He previously adapted to film the best-selling supernatural thriller novel *The Visitation* by author Frank Peretti for Ralph Winter (*X-Men, Wolverine*), and wrote and directed *Wall of Separation,* a PBS documentary, and *Lines That Divide,* a documentary on stem cell research.

Mr. Godawa's scripts have won multiple awards in respected screenplay competitions, and his articles on movies and philosophy have been published around the world. He has traveled around the United States teaching on movies, worldviews, and culture to colleges, churches and community groups.

His popular book, *Hollywood Worldviews: Watching Films with Wisdom and Discernment* (InterVarsity Press) is used as a textbook in schools around the country. His novel series, the saga *Chronicles of the Nephilim* is in the Top 10 of Biblical Fiction on Amazon and is an imaginative retelling of Biblical stories of the Nephilim giants, the secret plan of the fallen Watchers, and the War of the Seed of the Serpent with the Seed of Eve. The sequel series, *Chronicles of the Apocalypse* tells the story of the Apostle John's book of Revelation, and *Chronicles of the Watchers* recounts true history through the Watcher paradigm.

Find out more about his other books, lecture tapes and dvds for sale at his website www.godawa.com.

BLANK PAGE

BLANK PAGE

Made in United States
North Haven, CT
28 April 2025